W0006544

Unless otherwise indicated, Bible quotations are taken from the King James Version of the Bible.

POWERS

BEHIND THE SCENES

ARCHBISHOP N. DUNCAN-WILLIAMS

CONTENTS

Introduction

INTRODUCTION

"And my speech and my preaching was not with enticing words of man's wisdom, but in demonstration of the Spirit and of power: That your faith should not stand in the wisdom of men, but in the power of God. Howbeit we speak wisdom among them that are perfect: yet not the wisdom of this world, nor of the princes of this world, that come to nought: But we speak the wisdom of God in a mystery, even the hidden wisdom, which God ordained before the world unto our glory: Which none of the princes of this world knew: for had they known it, they would not have crucified the Lord of glory. But as it is written, Eye hath not seen, nor ear heard, neither have entered into the heart of man, the things which God hath prepared for them that love him. But God hath revealed them unto us by his Spirit: for the Spirit searcheth all things, yea, the deep things of God. For what man knoweth the things of a man, save the spirit of man which is in him? even so the things of God knoweth no man, but the Spirit of God. Now we have received, not the spirit of the world, but the spirit which is of God; that we might know the things that are freely given to us of God. Which things also we speak, not in the words which man's wisdom teacheth, but which the Holy Ghost teacheth; comparing spiritual things with spiritual. But the natural man receiveth not the things of the Spirit of God: for they are foolishness unto him: neither can he know them, because they are spiritually discerned. But he that is

spiritual judgeth all things, yet he himself is judged of no man." (1Corinthians 2:4-15)

Many people do not believe in the existence of an unseen realm and others try to operate in it yet do not understand it. In order to understand spiritual realms, we must understand realms of authority. Though there are many kinds of authority, spiritual authority is the greatest. If our authority in Christ is by the Spirit, it cannot be determined by a person's gender or race; there is no distinction between them in the spirit.

According to the Scripture in 1 Corinthians 2:4-15, spiritual things must be spiritually discerned! Intellect, science or anything that we can relate to in the natural will only distort man's view of what is going on in the spirit realm; we discern things spiritually by knowing them through our spirit man and not through our natural man.

Understanding realms of authority gives us a better foundation in understanding order. It is true that there is no male or female in the spirit, but there is always order. You do not have to worry about proving what you can do when you are subject to God's order because God's order always undergirds true authority, and that which He sets in place cannot be moved.

"For though we walk in the flesh, we do not war after the flesh: (For the weapons of our warfare are not carnal, but mighty through God to the pulling down of strongholds;" (2 Corinthians 10:3-4)

The authority of God, His will and desire for His people will always be challenged – this is a fact. The devil hates believers! Whether it is in the natural or the spirit realm, demonic forces will always fight against God's original intent for His people. The phrase "original intent" is very important and must be properly defined. "Original intent" is the sum of God's desires for His people and His expectations of them; that which has been appointed, set up and established by God, and though God has an original intent for man, it takes warfare to bring it to pass. This warfare however, is not in the natural and cannot be fought with enhanced sniper rifles, automatic grenade launchers or intercontinental ballistic missiles.

Although spiritual authority is the greatest, and the believer needs spiritual authority to enforce God's original intent, it often takes a back seat in the lives of men and is replaced by the more obvious or tangible realms of authority. Some people would give everything they have for religious authority, political authority or even the authority that comes with fame. Athletes draw from physical authority, while great minds lean on the authority of the intellectual realm. Rich people glean from their financial authority, and the people of the world cannot help but depend on their natural authority, but as Christians, we must rely solely on the spiritual authority, which we have through Christ Jesus.

Spiritual authority is the secret weapon of creation. Many people in high positions have tapped into this truth and those from the dark side crave authority in the spirit realm because they know that when harnessed and pushed, whether for good or for evil, it can rule over and affect every other realm that exists.

By making this point, I must note that there are two opposing kingdoms in the spirit realm, good vs. evil, darkness vs. light, the kingdom of our God vs. the kingdom of darkness. There is a battle going on in the spirit and it is not a natural one. The real battle is not over land, oil, political positions or the keys to the stock market. It is not over health, wealth or over any physical aspect of the life of an individual, but the real battle is over authority in the spirit, so the struggle and contentions over these physical aspects of man are only a result of the battle in the spirit. Every human being has the potential inside to rule and have dominion in the earth but there is an enemy on a mission to defeat the ability to realize this potential.

"Lest satan should get an advantage of us: for we are not ignorant of his devices." (2 Corinthians 2:11)

Powers Behind the Scenes was written to reveal the existence and the operations of the spirit realm and to expose and oppose satan's plan to dominate continents, nations, churches and individuals, especially believers. This book will give you keys that can help you live what should be a normal Christian life according to the will of God, and defeat satan and his demons and their work in your life.

-

Archbishop Nicholas Duncan Williams

CHAPTER ONE

THE

SPIRIT REALM

I woke up to an unfamiliar environment; my surroundings were very different from the last place I could remember. "Where am I, how did I get here?" I thought to myself. I could hear voices from a distance and the faint sound of the cry of babies. Then I smelled something quite familiar; disinfectant! I tried to move only to realize that I was firmly strapped to a bed. A woman appeared. She held my hand and exclaimed, "Nick, you missed death narrowly!" She was dressed in a nurse's uniform and it dawned on me… I was in a hospital.

The night immediately preceding that day in 1976 will forever be indelible in my mind and life. It produced marks that cannot be erased and are impossible for me to forget. That night, I could hardly sleep because of some strange happenings and I was under great strain and stress. I suffered hallucinations. A voice commanded me to light a candle in my bedroom. I obeyed. Then, the voice commanded me to stretch out my right palm over the flame. For some reason, I could not resist. My senses were lulled as some of my fingers roasted over the flame. Momentarily, I lost consciousness and all my actions were controlled by this strange voice.

Suddenly, my senses were restored. Sharp, agonizing sensations ripped through my body: I was in excruciating pain. As I looked down, I could not believe my eyes. My three middle fingers were burning! As they burned, blood spilled out profusely from the ends of what was left of them.

All alone in my room and unable to move, I screamed painfully for help using what little strength I had left inside me. The pain was so intense that my vision blurred. Then, I heard the sound of footsteps approaching my room and of my door being forced open. I must have passed out at that moment because I do not remember the events following the opening of the door; but somehow I woke up in ward eight of the Korle-Bu Teaching Hospital in Accra, Ghana the next morning.

How did I get there? "Why would anyone in their right mind burn their fingers?" you ask. I was not born again. I did not consider the church as a place of power and had consulted many mediums (diviners) in various places in Accra. As a result, I began to have strange visitations at night. I felt very haunted and tormented. Every night, I was hearing all kinds of voices making demands on me to commit suicide and do other weird things. It was on one of these nights that I was overwhelmed by one of those voices. The voice was not a human voice. It came from another realm—the spirit realm. It commanded me to put my natural fingers in the flame and I was under its spiritual control to obey.

9

The voice was not a human voice. It came from another realm—the spirit realm. It commanded me to put my natural fingers in the flame and I was under its spiritual control to obey.

Surprisingly, in a day and age when the world consults palm readers, psychics and horoscopes many Christians still have doubts and questions about the existence of the spirit realm—one that is not tangible and physical to us on earth. Some question whether the operations of other realms influence or even dictate the events and occurrences in the physical realm.

I can attest and declare through experience that this "other" realm is real. The activities and dealings of this other realm have an influence over every event in the natural. However, it is important to understand that we can regulate the power and influence of this realm.

This other realm is most commonly referred to as the spiritual or supernatural. The latter name depicts clearly how the spiritual realm has power and directly influences the physical.

In order to understand more clearly the workings of the spirit realm, we must first understand the composition of mankind.

"And the very God of peace sanctify you wholly; and I pray God your whole spirit and soul and body be preserved blameless unto the coming of our Lord Jesus Christ." (1 Thessalonians 5:23)

"And the Lord God formed man of the dust of the ground, and breathed into his nostrils the breath of life; and man became a living soul." (Genesis 2:7)

Man is a tri-partite being – spirit, soul and body. It is with his spirit that a man worships, and may contact God. The soul includes the conscious and subconscious mind, the realm of emotions and the will. The soul gives a man personality, self-awareness, rationality and a natural feeling. The body is a complex physical creation by which a person relates to this world and to other people in the world. Science has taught us that every person's body is in large measure a product of their DNA code, which exists in every cell of the body to program its amazing development. As marvelous as the body may be, man has a non-physical aspect that consists of a different kind of material – spirit. This part of man that is eternal.

Man is described as a living soul (Genesis 2:7), which came into being at first by the breath of God (Spirit) being breathed into a formation of the dust of the earth. Man is an intricate three-part being. For this reason, whatever happens in one part of a man's being has consequences in other areas of his being. For example, it is well known that a healthy, fit body is conducive to an upbeat attitude in the soul.

The Book of Proverbs states that, *"The spirit of a man will sustain his infirmity; but a wounded spirit who can bear?"* (Proverbs 18:14) and; *"A merry heart doeth good like a medicine: but a broken spirit drieth the bones."* (Proverbs 17:22). And this word is confirmed in Psalm 32, describing how unconfessed sin caused David's bones to grow old. *"Blessed is he whose transgression is forgiven, whose sin is covered. Blessed is the man unto whom the Lord imputeth not iniquity, and in whose spirit there is no guile. When I kept silence, my bones waxed old through my roaring all the day long."* (Psalm 32:1-3)

There are plenty of other examples that can be given of how all these aspects of man effect one another. It is a scientific fact. Obviously much valuable research could be done into the relationship between spirit, soul and body. Such research has its perils, of course, since when we start probing such deep mysteries without the guidance of the Holy Spirit, we may obtain knowledge and power that would bring forth the fruits of the tree of the knowledge of good and evil, and not of God's life. The whole study of psychology is something that needs to be brought under the Lordship of Jesus Christ and the authority of God's Word. If Christians simply refuse to get involved in this area and allow the ungodly to set the pace then much will be lost. On the other hand, to accept unquestioningly the teachings of psychology without the Spirit of God is to invite the shipwreck of our faith. Furthermore, the use of psychological principles divorced from a true submission to the Holy Spirit could result in powerful deception and the rejection of the Lord who bought us.

God is interested in all three portions of our being – spirit, soul and body. The Bible says concerning our Lord and Savior Jesus Christ; *"And Jesus increased in wisdom and stature, and in favour with God and man."* (Luke 2:52). This reveals the importance of our mental and emotional development, our physical prowess, our spiritual life with God, of worship and communion, and our social interactions with others. God is interested in all of these, and the Bible gives us keys for our development in these areas.

Never allow philosophers to confuse you by suggesting that God is the same as "the Universe". No, God stands outside of the Universe as well as inside it. He is the Creator of all things. He is not "one with all things" and neither are you, nor will you ever be. These "New Age" philosophies are just what the devil would want men to believe. In believing them, people don't only deny the existence of the devil which has deceived them, but also renounce their need for Jesus Christ as Savior and reject Him as Lord. In doing so, they reject the true Kingdom of God and become subjects in one of satan's worldly kingdoms.

God is not only Transcendent. He is "Immanent". That is to say, He is here. It is true that God is personally and actually within a true Christian believer. *"Examine yourselves, whether ye be in the faith; prove your own selves. Know ye not your own selves, how that Jesus Christ is in you, except ye be reprobates?"* (2 Corinthians 13:5) (See also Galatians 2:20 and 1 Corinthians 6:19). This is the truth. But again, do not be confused by those who say that God is "within us all". If He is, then the gospel of Jesus Christ as revealed in the Bible is a lie. The Bible reveals a need for man to be reconciled to God in one way only – and that is through faith in the shed blood of Jesus Christ, where Jesus became the ultimate sacrifice to bring us to God. To deny this is to call the truths of the Bible lies, in favor of the philosophies that trade in the souls of men to their eternal destruction.

One thing is the desire of the Holy Spirit for us, and the other is the way our own souls would seek to go about fulfilling our needs, wants and desires. Paul the apostle referred to the latter way as "the flesh". Paul indicates; *"For the flesh lusteth against the Spirit, and the Spirit against the flesh: and these are contrary the one to the other: so that ye cannot do the things that ye would."* (Galatians 5:17).

The key to successful Christian living is actually to learn to progressively renounce our own soulish devices and allow our minds to be retrained by the Holy Spirit. This can be very painful, and leads to an actual and ongoing "death" or "crucifixion of the flesh" – to use biblical language. Yet the fruit of it is the very peace we are craving as a foundation for our emotional existence. We also find the revelation of the love of God toward us and through us as we learn to submit to the Holy Spirit. *"But the fruit of the Spirit is love, joy, peace, longsuffering, gentleness, goodness, faith,*

Meekness, temperance: against such there is no law. And they that are Christ's have crucified the flesh with the affections and lusts." (Galatians 5:22-24). The Holy Spirit will also empower us to reveal a portion of the attributes of God through the gifts of the Holy Spirit. This is a definite part of the plan of God for every true child of God. The denial of this has robbed the Body of Christ of more than it can imagine. We claim that God lives in us. Why is so little happening then?

Our spirit, souls and bodies need to be offered to God. This does not take away our responsibility before God, neither our will. Every day is an opportunity to embrace the cross and to experience the resurrection. "Faith" and "love" will lead us to do so every time.

With all my life's experiences before and after I became born-again, coupled with over 38 years in ministry and above all, the undeniable truth of the word of God, I am highly persuaded that there are unseen forces that operate in the earth to influence and affect the events of the lives of men.

Those forces work against all aspects of man—his spirit, soul and his body. Before you address the powers behind the scene, you must understand more fully those aspects of who you are and God's will for each aspect of your life.

CHAPTER TWO

GOD'S PLAN FOR MAN

God created man in His image and likeness, blessed them (male and female) and give them a dominion mandate (Genesis 1:26-28) to subdue the earth. The serpent entered that garden, deceived Eve and took away from Adam the glory of that dominion. Now, Jesus had redeemed it for us but we must enforce our dominion on the earth using the authority of His name.

God's plan for Adam and Eve was a life of blessing—one without sickness, disease, infirmity, poverty, lack or weariness. Yet we see these evils occurring frequently in the lives of believers. What is going on? Why is this happening? Well, in order to diagnose properly what went wrong, we first need to understand what the "normal" status of man was intended to be. Let us consider God's will our bodies, spirits and souls—the state of these aspects of our being when free from the influence of satan's powers behind the scenes. We begin with our bodies.

God's Will for Our Bodies

I want to mention three things that are clearly God's will for our bodies. Getting this right will make a tremendous difference to our spiritual, as well as our emotional life and help to identify the workings of powers behind the scenes.

Sexual Purity

"For this is the will of God, even your sanctification, that ye should abstain from fornication: That every one of you should know how to possess his vessel in sanctification and honour; Not in the lust of concupiscence, even as the Gentiles which know not God:... For God hath not called us unto uncleanness, but unto holiness. He therefore that despiseth, despiseth not man, but God, who hath also given unto us his holy Spirit." (1Thesalonians 4:3-5, 7-8).

If sexual purity was not so important, satan would not work so hard to destroy it wherever he can find people who will sell out. Sexual purity is important for our communion with God. God definitely wants Christians to abstain from adultery and fornication as well as the more serious sexual sins such as sodomy. To refuse to do so is to reject God. It is a lie to think that what we do with our bodies does not affect our souls or our spirits or that the spirit realm cannot influence what we do with our bodies

Physical Wealth

"Beloved, I wish above all things that thou mayest prosper and be in health, even as thy soul prospereth." (3John 1:2).

The apostle John was praying for prosperity for the church. Many believers have a confused mindset about prosperity. They believe that prosperity is a carnal and materialistic goal but this is one of the lies of the devil. This is what the prophet Zachariah said; *"... Thus saith the Lord of hosts; My cities through prosperity shall yet be spread abroad;*

... " (Zachariah 1:17). The church must prosper in order to be able to reach the ends of the earth with the good news of the Gospel. Prosperity according to the word of God means, *"...having all sufficiency in all things at all times that one may abound to every good work."* (2 Corinthians 9:8)

This is what the prophet Zachariah said; "... Thus saith the Lord of hosts; My cities through prosperity shall yet be spread abroad; ..." (Zachariah 1:17). The church must prosper in order to be able to reach the ends of the earth with the good news of the Gospel.

Physical Health

In 3 John 1:2, the Apostle Paul does not only mention physical prosperity but the need for Christians to be in "good health."

Many Scriptures indicate that God's will is for us to have healthy bodies. Sickness is a result of the fall and is the specialty of satan. Jesus healed *"all who were oppressed by the devil"* (Acts 10:38) and even those whom his disciples failed to heal, such as the boy with the epilepsy in Matthew 17:14-21. This indicates that even when Christians cannot get someone healed because of unbelief (vs 20), it is still the will of God to heal them. It is a bitter pill for Christians and ministers to hear that their unbelief is preventing God's miracles, but it is very relevant.

Physical Fitness

"For bodily exercise profiteth little: but godliness is profitable unto all things, having promise of the life that now is, and of that which is to come." (1 Timothy 4:8).

Let's not forget that Jesus worked as a carpenter and would have been physically strong. This in part enabled him to fast 40 days. Paul went through a lot physically and I am sure he trained his body. He said that he buffeted his body and brought it into subjection; *"But I keep under my body, and bring it into subjection: lest that by any means, when I have preached to others, I myself should be a castaway."* (1 Corinthians 9:27). If we don't strengthen our bodies through exercise, they will go to sleep on us when we need to be alert or diligent. They will also create in our souls a kind of depression, which taints our being and makes us less attractive as Christians.

If we don't strengthen our bodies through exercise, they will go to sleep on us when we need to be alert or diligent. They will also create in our souls a kind of depression, which taints our being and makes us less attractive as Christians.

God's Will for Our Souls

"Finally, brethren, whatsoever things are true, whatsoever things are honest, whatsoever things are just, whatsoever things are pure, whatsoever things are lovely, whatsoever things are of good report; if there be any virtue, and if there be any praise, think on these things." (Philippians 4:8)

God wants us to think on good things. This word needs to be taken seriously. There is a considerable scope for freedom and latitude in this instruction. Our minds should be on Jesus–He is all those things, and by filling our minds with the Word of God we can do this also. However, there are many good things in this world we can meditate on: things in nature, things in people and of purpose that we may find or read of from time to time. These things are the gifts of God to us, and God wants us to meditate on them– to feed our subconscious minds with them. This will help us become happy people.

God wants us to think on good things. These things are the gifts of God to us, and God wants us to meditate on them–to feed our subconscious minds with them. This will help us become happy people.

Once you know your particular life calling from God, it is good to study and ponder all good and noble things which relate especially to this calling. *"For as he thinketh in his heart, so is he: ..."* (Proverbs 23:7). We often spend much of our time worrying when we should be praising God and thinking on good things. It requires effort to discipline the mind; but truly, the results are worth it. Strangely, physical discipline can be a major key also to disciplining the mind. Whenever the mind is uncontrollably focused on bad (not good) things, powers behind the scenes—supernatural powers—are in operation.

The Spiritual Life

The Bible tells us, "Be continually filled with the Holy Spirit." That is God's will for us. It is a serious sin actually to neglect this commandment of God. It is impossible to maintain this fullness without developing a life of prayer as well as the discipline of quieting the soul and waiting upon the Lord.

Meditation on the Word feeds both our spirit and soul. The more you repeat one small portion of Scripture to yourself, the more profoundly it will impact you. Many Christians, , have a far greater breadth of intellectual knowledge concerning God's word, than true heart knowledge of what the Word was pointing us to in Jesus. Biblical meditation, repeating, muttering and thinking on one thing repetitively, is a key to prosperity and success (see Joshua 1:8; Psalm 1:1-3). Psychologically and neurologically, it has been proven scientifically that repetition of a phrase causes more parts of the brain to be used. This shows it is entering into us more deeply. If you trust the Word of God, allow it to enter deeply into you through meditation.

The Inner Witness of the Human Spirit

God's Spirit does not always tell us what we need to do by means of an inner voice. We can get into trouble if we demand or expect God's voice to come immediately in answer to our questions, especially if we are not in an attitude of true spiritual worship and waiting upon God. And I must say, though I am a prophet of God, even unto nations, we cannot afford to allow our life direction to be guided by prophetic words from others. These generally strengthen but do not initiate the purposes of God in our lives.

We will do better, as Christians, if we learn to listen to the inner witness of our own regenerated human spirits. *"The spirit of man is the candle of the Lord, searching all the inward parts of the belly."* (Proverbs 20:27). Your spirit knows things that your mind does not. The Holy Spirit knows even more than our human spirits, and can enlighten us on any matter if He wishes to speak to us, as long as we are listening to Him. However, generally it is through the regenerated spirit of man that we know the way to go on a particular issue.

These are just some of the plans of God for the lives of His people. God wants us to dwell in peace. The sum of His intentions for man is found in the book of Genesis;

"So God created man in his own image, in the image of God created he him; male and female created he them. And God blessed them, and God said unto them, Be fruitful, and multiply, and replenish the earth, and subdue it: and have dominion over the fish of the sea, and over the fowl of the air, and over every living thing that moveth upon the earth. And God said, Behold, I have given you every herb bearing seed, which is upon the face of all the earth, and every tree, in the which is the fruit of a tree yielding seed; to you it shall be for meat. And to every beast of the earth, and to every fowl of the air, and to every thing that creepeth upon the earth, wherein there is life, I have given every green herb for meat: and it was so." (Genesis 1:27-30).

This in fact was a command, not a conditional promise or blessing. God created man and gave him authority to possess and have dominion over everything pertaining to the earth realm.

One may ask, if this was God's command, why is there so much suffering and hardship among the human race? This is because man sinned and seeded his authority to satan. Now in order for man to walk in the commanded blessing, he has to fight for it.

"For we wrestle not against flesh and blood, but against principalities, against powers, against the rulers of the darkness of this world, against spiritual wickedness in high places." (Ephesians 6:12)

23

Scripture makes it clear that regardless of what the challenges or struggles and even conquest in life may be, there are always unseen beings and persons without bodies influencing natural acts and occurrences. Although these things manifest in the flesh, whether they are victories or defeats, falls or triumph, the outcome is not determined by the activities of our flesh or our natural realm but spiritual forces that operate through flesh and blood. The issues we face in life, though they are tangible, are not controlled or influenced by natural elements but by a very sophisticated organization of spirits. Until believers come to the realization and understanding of spiritual forces behind the scenes, we will fight the wrong enemy with the right weapons and the right enemy with the wrong weapons.

In Ephesians 6, Apostle Paul made an attempt to take our focus and attention off the natural scene and asked believers to take a step and switch from the natural to the supernatural and stop identifying the wrong enemy. In other words, he was telling us to stop dealing with branches, leaves and fruits and get to the roots. We have to take our eyes off the natural and look into the spirit.

Until believers come to the realization and understanding of spiritual forces behind the scenes, we will fight the wrong enemy with the right weapons and the right enemy with the wrong weapons.

Certain diseases cannot be diagnosed by medical questions and answers but require the use of special diagnostic equipment in order to locate and identify exactly what is responsible for a particular condition. Only then, can the right treatment be given to a patient. In the same way, we need to switch from natural tools and use the weapons of the spirit to diagnose spiritual conditions.

Apostle Paul said; *"Lest satan should get an advantage of us: for we are not ignorant of his devices."* (2 Corinthians 2:11).

Spiritual kingdoms are defended by spiritual weapons.

CHAPTER THREE

TWO

OPPOSING KINGDOMS

SATAN'S KINGDOM

The Bible reveals that satan is a created being; therefore, he was, and still is subject to the Creator. He was originally called Lucifer, meaning "the light bearer," derived from the words "lucem ferre." This word translates in Hebrew as "morning star." In many translations, Lucifer means radiant, shiny, and ambient being.

"Son of man, take up a lamentation upon the king of Tyrus, and say unto him, Thus saith the Lord God; Thou sealest up the sum, full of wisdom, and perfect in beauty. Thou hast been in Eden the garden of God; every precious stone was thy covering, the sardius, topaz, and the diamond, the beryl, the onyx, and the jasper, the sapphire, the emerald, and the carbuncle, and gold: the workmanship of thy tabrets and of thy pipes was prepared in thee in the day that thou wast created. Thou art the anointed cherub that covereth; and I have set thee so: thou wast upon the holy mountain of God; thou hast walked up and down in the midst of the stones of fire. Thou wast perfect in thy ways from the day that thou wast created, till iniquity was found in thee. By the multitude of thy merchandise they have filled the midst of thee with violence, and thou hast sinned:

therefore I will cast thee as profane out of the mountain of God: and I will destroy thee, O covering cherub, from the midst of the stones of fire. Thine heart was lifted up because of thy beauty, thou hast corrupted thy wisdom by reason of thy brightness: I will cast thee to the ground, I will lay thee before kings, that they may behold thee. Thou hast defiled thy sanctuaries by the multitude of thine iniquities, by the iniquity of thy traffic; therefore will I bring forth a fire from the midst of thee, it shall devour thee, and I will bring thee to ashes upon the earth in the sight of all them that behold thee. All they that know thee among the people shall be astonished at thee: thou shalt be a terror, and never shalt thou be any more". (Ezekiel 28:12-19)

When satanwas created, he was an angel of God; one of the cherubim class of angels; holy, wise, beautiful and perfect as scripture describes him. He was the leader amongst the cherubs and was referred to as "covering cherub." He was given the ability to reflect the glory of God more than any other created being.

Though satanwas a powerful angel, he did not retain the position that was given to him by God. He became perverted and rebellious and not only turned his back on his creator but also attempted to take His place. He fell through pride and selfishness by thinking of himself higher than he ought.

In the Bible, we see a clear contradiction between the nature of satan and the nature of our Lord and Savior Jesus Christ, who we live to exemplify:

"Let this mind be in you, which was also in Christ Jesus: Who, being in the form of God, thought it not robbery to be equal with God: But made himself of no reputation, and took upon him the form of a servant, and was made in the likeness of men: And being found in fashion as a man, he humbled himself, and became obedient unto death, even the death of the cross. Wherefore God also hath highly exalted him, and given him a name which is above every name: That at the name of Jesus every knee should bow, of things in heaven, and things in earth, and things under the earth; And that every tongue should confess that Jesus Christ is Lord, to the glory of God the Father." (Philippians 2:5-11).

Jesus Christ walked on the earth as a mere mortal even though He was God. He humbled Himself and was not carried away by the praises of men and the power He possessed. On the other hand, the Bible shows us how conceited satan was: all he thought about was himself and all that he possessed. This is what Jesus warns us of when He said, *"Take heed, and beware of covetousness: for a man's life consisteth not in the abundance of the things which he possesseth."* (Luke 12:15).

In the book of Isaiah, we see the extent of satan's conceit and negative ambition that led to his fall. One of my fathers in the faith, Lester Sumrall refers to them as "the five foolish and fatal 'I wills' of Lucifer."

"How art thou fallen from heaven, O Lucifer, son of the morning! how art thou cut down to the ground, which didst weaken the nations! For thou hast said in thine heart, I will ascend into heaven, I will exalt my throne above the stars of God: I will sit also upon the mount of the congregation, in the sides of the north: I will ascend above the heights of the clouds; I will be like the most High." (Isaiah 14:12-14).

The phrase "I will" by satan occurs five times in three verses of scripture. He desired five main things; to occupy God's abode in heaven and obtain equal recognition with God, to wield Gods' rule over the angels, to rule the earth, to take God's glory for himself and lastly to possess everything that belonged to God.

Because of his dubious and deceptive nature, satandid not fall alone. He lured one-third of Gods' angels through his lies and the abuse of the office that God gave him in heaven. These angels backed satan in his rebellion against God. Their rebellion caused a war in heaven and as a result, they all fell with him.

This "I will" nature can also be identified in the lives of men. For example, it is evident that the King of Tyre referred to in Ezekiel 28 was not a human being. Even though there was a natural ruler who was mortal, a spiritual ruler influenced his rule. The scripture uses a dual reference. It reveals just how satan operates. The natural ruler was merely an actor in a movie written and directed by the spiritual ruler or, the natural ruler was a robot remotely controlled by the spiritual ruler, Lucifer. This revelation gives us another perspective on the laws and decrees of some governments and shows us that there are unseen personalities that influence and even control many situations in the natural.

The natural ruler was merely an actor in a movie written and directed by the spiritual ruler or, the natural ruler was a robot remotely controlled by the spiritual ruler, Lucifer.

Scripture defines clearly satan's titles, abilities, and influence. In the Scriptures, he is identified by various designations, including names, titles, descriptions and animal-like representations, which, in themselves, tell quite a lot about him.

THE ORIGINAL NATURE OF SATAN

In reference to the one we commonly call satan and the devil, Scripture assigns him no negative designation in his original, sinless state, only positive ones. They are:

The Anointed Cherub

Ezekiel 28:14 begins, "thou art the anointed cherub that covereth...." Verse 16 calls him, "O covering cherub..." As to the nature of his spirit body, satan was a cherub, and always will be.

Cherubs are beings of sublime and celestial nature, which have a particular station or office. During the expulsion of Adam and Eve from the Garden of Eden, their office was to prevent all access to the tree of life—to keep watch. Later in Scripture, they also form the throne and chariot of Jehovah in his manifestation of himself on earth. He dwelleth between and sitteth on the cherubim (1Sa 4:4; Psa 80:1; Eze 1:26,28). (Easton's Bible Dictionary).

One of the responsibilities of a covering cherub is to keep guard or to watch. Satan continues to watch, seeking whom he might devour and what accusations he can bring against the believers day and night. He still carries a certain perverted glory that seduces and deceives many into worshipping at his throne.

Day-Star and Son of the Morning.

These two designations appear in Isaiah 14:12: "How art thou fallen from heaven, O day-star, son of the morning!"

In addition to his special anointing, which we'll consider shortly, Ezekiel 28:12 reveals how he was the shining one: "Son of man, lift up a lament over the king of Tyre, and say to him, So says the Lord Jehovah: You seal the measure, full of wisdom and perfect in beauty."

He was the shining one by virtue of his special anointing and by the fact that he was filled to angelic capacity with wisdom and perfection in angelic beauty."

The Anointed Cherub that Covers

Ezekiel 28:14 begins; "Thou art the anointed cherub that covers".... In Ezekiel 10:1, we see the throne of God hovering above the cherubim; *"Then I looked, and, behold, in the firmament that was above the head of the cherubims there appeared over them as it were a sapphire stone, as the appearance of the likeness of a throne."* But in 28:14, we see the Shining One covering, or hovering above, or spread out over, the throne of God. His having been anointed shows that He was especially endowed by God for his breathtakingly glorious role as the covering cherub.

This title also reveals a second position held by this cherub. Cherubim are the highest order of angel, and this cherub was *The Anointed Cherub*, indicating that he had preeminence over all other cherubim and all the seraphim and rank and file angels, as well. In other words, he had preeminence over the entire angelic host.

Ezekiel 28:13b reveals yet another facet of his position as *The Anointed Cherub that Covers*: "The workmanship of your tambourines and of your flutes was prepared in you in the day that you were created."

These musical instruments were in him as he hovered above God, above the seraphim (Isaiah 6:2) and above the other cherubim (Ezekiel 10:1). These scriptures paint the picture of a worship leader who led the entire company of angels in the worship of God.

To sum up, three positions are included in the title *The Anointed Cherub that Covers*:

He hovered above the throne of God, he had preeminence over the entire angelic host and he led the entire company of angels in the heavenly worship of God. He was created beautiful and decorated with precious stones and minerals. Bible scholars believe that satan was in charge of worship in heaven and was the first created being with musical ability. He embodied musical instruments. He did not need a musical instrument or someone to play it, he was an all-in-one musical instrument and he had mastered the use of himself. *"... the workmanship of thy tabrets and of thy pipes was prepared in thee in the day that thou wast created."* (Ezekiel 28:13) It is therefore not a surprise to see how satan has used music as a means of luring souls.

He hovered above the throne of God, he had preeminence over the entire angelic host and he led the entire company of angels in the heavenly worship of God.

Ezekiel 28 also reveals that satan was a merchant or trader. *"By the multitude of thy merchandise they have filled the midst of thee with violence, and thou hast sinned:"* (Ezekiel 28:16). Derek Prince explains this attribute of satan in his book entitled, *Lucifer Exposed:*

"Now let us examine a fascinating word that appears in this passage: "trading." In Hebrew it means, "to go up and down as a talebearer, as an agitator, with secret underhanded agitation." Today we call it campaigning or lobbying. That is how Lucifer alienated the loyalty of the angels: by going back and forth, declaring, in effect, "Look at me. See how beautiful and intelligent I am? Don't you think I'd make a better ruler than God up there? And you know, God doesn't really appreciate you, if you'll join me, I'll give you a much higher position in my kingdom than you have at present time.""

He adds, "Let's look at some of the uses of the word trading in order to see the accuracy of its description, *"You shall not go about as a talebearer among your people"* (Leviticus 19:16). This verse describes a slanderer, a person bringing false insinuations and accusations. Lucifer falsely accused God of being a despot, a tyrant who only cared for His own grandeur and glory, with no appreciation of these angels who were so faithfully serving Him.""

Satan's abilities and possessions caused his heart to be lifted with pride. The reasons for his fall are the very weapons he deploys against man today. The first sin that took place was the sin of pride and it was not committed here on earth but in heaven, not by an ordinary being but a "cherub that covereth." If a cherub committed the sin of pride, what chance do mere mortals stand against its temptation?

The sin of pride is often called the sin of sins. It was this sin, which transformed Lucifer, an anointed cherub of God, the very "seal of perfection, full of wisdom and perfect in beauty", into satan, the devil, the father of lies, the one for whom hell itself was created. And we are warned to guard our hearts against pride lest we too "fall into the same condemnation as the devil."

It was the lust of the flesh, the lust of the eyes and the sin of pride that first led Eve to eat of the forbidden fruit. In Genesis we read, *"Then the serpent said to the woman, And the serpent said unto the woman, Ye shall not surely die: For God doth know that in the day ye eat thereof, then your eyes shall be opened, and ye shall be as gods, knowing good and evil. And when the woman saw that the tree was good for food, and that it was pleasant to the eyes, and a tree to be desired to make one wise, she took of the fruit thereof, and did eat, and gave also unto her husband with her; and he did eat"* (Genesis 3:4-6). Satan, the serpent, eager to share his condemnation with man, introduced Eve to the sin of pride. He himself had transitioned from archangel Lucifer to satan by this sin so he was well acquainted with it.

The sin of pride is often called the sin of sins. It was this sin, which transformed Lucifer, an anointed cherub of God, the very "seal of perfection, full of wisdom and perfect in beauty", into satan, the devil, the father of lies, the one for whom hell itself was created.

WAR IN HEAVEN

Satan's pride stirred up war in heaven and as a result, he was cast out into the earth.

"And there was war in heaven: Michael and his angels fought against the dragon; and the dragon fought and his angels, And prevailed not; neither was their place found any more in heaven. And the great dragon was cast out, that old serpent, called the Devil, and Satan, which deceiveth the whole world: he was cast out into the earth, and his angels were cast out with him." (Revelations 12:7-9).

Pride caused war in heaven and pride is still the cause of many wars and conflicts in our world today. The war in heaven was an uprising of satan against the order and protocol of heaven. Michael, who we can refer to in this case as the defense minister of heaven, and his subordinates fought against Lucifer and his subordinates. Even though the rebellion was against God, the Father, the Son and the Holy Spirit, did not get involved in the battle because it is below the dignity of the Creator to fight His creation.

Engaging in direct battle with His creation would have diminished God's authority. Isaiah 45:9 says *"Woe unto him that striveth with his Maker! Let the potsherd strive with the potsherds of the earth..."* God therefore cast satan into the earth because just like man, he was also created by God. Revelations 12 also reveals that satan was indeed cast into the earth; *"... Woe to the inhabiters of the earth and of the sea! for the devil is come down unto you, having great wrath, because he knoweth that he hath but a short time."* (Revelations 12:12).

The earth is not satan's final destination, according to Isaiah 14; *"Yet thou shalt be brought down to hell, to the sides of the pit."* (Isaiah 14:15) He is destined for the lake of fire together with his fallen angels and all who yield to him.

"And I saw an angel come down from heaven, having the key of the bottomless pit and a great chain in his hand. And he laid hold on the dragon, that old serpent, which is the Devil, and Satan ... (who) was cast into the lake of fire and brimstone ... and shall be tormented day and night for ever and ever." (Revelation 20:1-3, 10)

The Present Nature of Satan

Satan is not a red-skinned humanlike creature with a checkered jacket, horns, forked tail and pitchfork stoking up the flames of hell and tormenting its inhabitants. This is a myth except for the fact that he'll be there.

HIS BASIC NATURE

Cherub

As noted, Ezekiel 28:14 identifies satan as a cherub, and a cherub he still is and always will be.

The Evil One

This title is found in Matthew 6:13, John 17:15, 2 Thessalonians 3:3 and 1 John 5:18-19. According to Strong's, the Greek word for evil here is *poneyros*, which means evil in influence or effect. The title indicates that he is totally evil in everything he influences and does.

Satan

This name of *The Evil One* is found over fifty times in the Scriptures, and means adversary. Because he is *The Evil One*, he is the adversary of God, God's ways, God's works and God's people, and indeed, of all people. 1 Chronicles 21:1 shows an example of his adversarial stance against the people of God: "And satan stood up against Israel, and moved David to number Israel."

HIS GOALS

Destroyer, Abaddon, Apollyon

This title appears in Revelation 9:11: And they had a king over them, the angel of the bottomless pit, whose name in the Hebrew tongue is Abaddon, but in Greek his name is Apollyon. Abaddon (Hebrew) and Apollyon (Greek) mean Destroyer. This Destroyer is named king over the horrible locusts of Revelation 9:1-10 that will ascend from the bottomless pit. These "locusts" were actually demons, and Destroyer, their king, is most likely satan. (The high ranking demons over Greece and Persia were called princes, not kings [Daniel 10:13, 20]). Destroyer speaks of his efforts at destroying God's plans, works and people.

A Roaring Lion

1 Peter 5:8 says, your adversary, the Devil, walks about like a roaring lion, seeking someone he may devour;

This, too, portrays satan as a destroyer of people. In context, it specifically portrays him as a destroyer of the faith and the walk of believers.

MODES OF OPERATION

The Tempter

Found in Matthew 4:3 and 1 Thessalonians 3:5, this designation shows satan as the one who entices people to sin. Matthew 4:3: "And when the tempter came to him, he said, 'If thou be the Son of God, command that these stones be made bread.'"

The Deceiver

This designation is found in Revelation 12:9, in which satan is called, the deceiver of the whole world, showing him as the one who, by deception, beguiles the great mass of humanity into rejecting God and His ways. As often as he is able, he even deceives believers into rejecting God's good counsel, which is why Ephesians 6:11 exhorts us to stand against the wiles of the devil.

The Angel of Light.

"And no marvel; for Satan himself is transformed into an angel of light." (2Corinthians 11:14)

This scripture shows that satan carries out the work of deception by offering appealing counterfeits of true moral and spiritual understanding, of which this *kosmos* abounds in its legion of false religions, philosophies, beliefs and opinions.

The Devil.

Devil means Accuser or Slanderer, and declares the chief way he seeks to cause division between God and His people, and between God's people. It is used only in the New Testament, and is found there thirty-five times.

The Accuser of the Brethren.

Revelation 12: designates satan as the accuser of believers. *"And I heard a loud voice saying in heaven, Now is come salvation, and strength, and the kingdom of our God, and the power of his Christ: for the accuser of our brethren is cast down, which accused them before our God day and night".* (Revelations 12:10) and we see him in action against Job; *"Then satan answered the Lord, and said, Doth Job fear God for nought? Hast not thou made an hedge about him, and about his house, and about all that* he hath on every side? thou hast blessed the work of his hands, and his substance is increased in the land. But put forth thine hand now, and touch all that he hath, and he will curse thee to thy face" (Job 1:9-11) and also in Job 2:5 which says; "But put forth thine hand now, and touch his bone and his flesh, and he will curse thee to thy face."

HOW HE EMPLOYS HIS MEANS

The Serpent

Satan is depicted as a serpent in about ten places in the Bible, most notably in Genesis 3:1, the first reference to him in Scripture. This depiction brings to mind his cleverness and cunning in deception, as in his temptation of Eve: "Now the serpent was more cunning than any beast of the field which Jehovah God had made."

The Dragon

Satan is portrayed as a dragon in Revelation 12, emphasizing the great power and ferocity he employed in his attempt to devour the Child of the woman (Revelation 12:4; Matthew 2), and will employ to destroy the woman, Israel, who gave birth to the Child (Revelation 12:13).

The Present Positions of Satan In Relation to Other Demons

The Prince of Demons

This title is found in Matthew 12:24 and Luke 11:15, and obviously shows his authority over all other demons.

The Prince of the Powers of the Air

This title is found in Ephesians 2:2, and likewise shows that satan, who presently abides in the atmosphere, is the ruler of his subordinate powers of the air, the demons, who also abide in the atmosphere.

IN THE PRESENT WORLD SYSTEM

The God of This Age

This title is found in 2 Corinthians 4:4, and emphasizes satan's control of this age; whose worldview is so contrary to that of Jesus Christ.

The Prince of This World.

This designation appears in John 12:31, 14:30, and 16:11. In each case, the Greek word for world is *kosmos*, which refers to our world system in regards to its prevailing satanic spirit and the way that it's consequently arranged and conducted, as opposed to the Spirit of the Kingdom of God and the way that it is arranged and conducted.

The King of Babylon

This title is found in Isaiah 14:4 and, viewed in the context of verses 4-17, metaphorically portrays satan as in control of all worldly kingdoms.

The King of Tyre

This title is found in Ezekiel 28:11-12 and, viewed in the context of verses 11-19, likewise metaphorically portrays satan as the demon king of all earthly kingdoms.

SOME BIBLICAL VIEWS CONCERNING SATAN

Belial.

Belial is found in 2 Corinthians 6:15 where it says; *"And what concord hath Christ with Belial? or what part hath he that believeth with an infidel?"* Belial means "worthlessness" and describes satan's net value in God's eyes in terms of his ability to be or do anything good and also that after all his to and fro and trying to destroy God's people, his end in hell has already been determined. Nevertheless, Scripture reveals that he, as well as the other demons, are worthy of respect, even as criminals about to be executed are normally handled with dignity in countries having a biblical heritage.

Belial depicts satan as the ruling spiritual wickedness, and has a host of wicked spirits that operate under his authority. The name Belial comes from a Hebrew word, "Beliiyual", which means without profit, worthlessness, destruction, wickedness, and mighty evil stubbornness. The work of this spirit is to cause men to commit contemptible and vile sins—sins that are so vile as to rouse moral indignation.

All sin is sin, but some sins are more abominable than others. When Belial is in control of a family, rape, incest, and sodomy can be found running in the family. These sins seem to have an unbreakable control over that family.

The Bible compares the sons of Belial to thorns that cannot be handled or taken with the hands.

"But the sons of Belial shall be all of them as thorns thrust away, because they cannot be taken with hands: But the man that shall touch them must be fenced with iron and the staff of a spear; and they shall be utterly burned with fire in the same place." (2Samuel 23:6-7)

The latter part of this Scripture says that they who can conquer these spirits "must be fenced with iron." The iron here refers to the whole armor of God. It is completely impossible to deal with this spirit with human strength. Beloved, is any member of your family under the influence of such a strong man? Jail will not solve the problem. Medicine will be of little help in surpassing the outward symptoms. Total freedom of this spiritual strong man comes only by putting on the whole armor of God, taking the Word of God—the sword of the Spirit, and enforcing it.

Beelzebub

Beelzebub means Lord of the Flies, and is found in Matthew 10:25; 12:24, 27; Mark 3:22; and Luke 11:15, 18,

19. It is a comical term for satan employed by the rabbis of Jesus' day. Beelzebub is a play on "Beelzebul," the Greek form of the original Philistine name, which means Lord of the Royal Palace.

It is important for us to understand that although satan and his angels fell, they did not lose their power and abilities because *"... the gifts and calling of God are without repentance."* (Romans 11:29) Satan still possesses all the gifts,talents and abilities with which God created him. Therefore, it is important for Christians to understand the rules of engagement and spiritual authority. It is for this reason that when satan contended with Michael over the body of Moses, Michael did not bring a charge against him; *"Yet Michael the archangel, when contending with the devil he disputed about the body of Moses, durst not bring against him a railing accusation, but said, The Lord rebuke thee."*(Jude 1:9).

Even though Michael defeated satan in heaven, he could not fight him on earth because in the earth satan matched him in rank because he was a fallen archangel. Michael therefore called upon the LORD to rebuke satan.

Satan and his fallen angels are currently working on earth to turn as many people against God as possible. He accuses man to God and accuses God to man. Because he is not omnipresent (present everywhere) and omniscient (all – knowing) it must be understood that the vast majority of all demonic activity is carried out by his subordinates and not by satan himself. Most times when we say that satan did a particular work, what it means is that he is the motivation behind the work and not that he carried out or committed the act by himself. He is a master networker and he works through a vast organization of spirit beings who are united towards one goal and purpose-- to undermine the human encounter with the Kingdom of God and oppose every will of God concerning the lives of humans. They attempt to gain influence over government leaders, and areas like education by inspiring satanic policies to achieve their goal. For our purposes, we can establish that most evil acts are carried out by satan's subordinates unless Scripture specifically identifies satan as the one personally carrying out a specific activity; however we must remember that satan is the inspiration and motivation behind all evil regardless of who carries it out. The spirit beings who work alongside satan are personalities we refer to as "evil spirits" or demons.

There are also some spirits that are representative of, and characterize satan;

Behemoth

"His scales are his pride, shut up together as with a close seal. One is so near to another, that no air can come between them. They are joined one to another, they stick together, that they cannot be sundered. By his neesings a light doth shine, and his eyes are like the eyelids of the morning. Out of his mouth go burning lamps, and sparks of fire leap out. Out of his nostrils goeth smoke, as out of a seething pot or caldron. His breath kindleth coals, and a

flame goeth out of his mouth. In his neck remaineth strength, and sorrow is turned into joy before him. The flakes of his flesh are joined together: they are firm in themselves; they cannot be moved. His heart is as firm as a stone; yea, as hard as a piece of the nether millstone." (Job 41:15-24)

This spirit characterizes satan and is responsible for the control of some of the systems and religions that oppress multitudes of people. The control can be over political or religious systems. Behemoths must be bound and their strongholds plundered to release people to come to Christ. Persistent prayer and corporate fasting can break Behemoth's powers. The Scripture cited above discloses the strength of this spirit, which must not be underestimated.

Leviathan

Following the above account in Scripture, we are told of another powerful spirit who appears invincible. (Job 41:1-34). Leviathan is represented in Scripture as a crocodile, a crooked serpent, and a dragon. He characterizes satan.

Leviathan promotes wickedness in various forms. This spirit also hardens the hearts of men against God and causes them to walk in pride. Pride is to seek to be independent of God and to walk in self-deception, or to have an exaggerated impression of one's self. People under the influence of this strong man are very resistant to the gospel. They will maintain a religious gap and be sources of rebellion against spiritual authority.

Reading the whole of Job 41, one discovers the incredible adamancy and strongholds of these spirit beings, Behemoth and Leviathan. The answer to paralyzing the enemy lies in the book of the prophet Isaiah.

"In that day the Lord with His severe sword, great and strong, will punish Leviathan the fleeing serpent, Leviathan the twisted serpent; and He will slay the reptile that is in the sea." (Isaiah 27:1)

"In that day" in the above Scripture refers to "the day of awakening," when the children of God will rise up to exercise their divine rights. Please note that the only weapon used in this combat will be the sword of the Lord—the Word of God.

CHAPTER FOUR

HIERARCHIES AND OPERATIONS

OF

SATAN'S KINGDOM

Many believe that demons are the wicked spirits of dead men. Yet Jesus tells a story in the Bible, of a rich man who died, was being tormented and was not able to come back to earth.

"And he said, Nay, father Abraham: but if one went unto them from the dead, they will repent. And he said unto him, If they hear not Moses and the prophets, neither will they be persuaded, though one rose from the dead." (Luke 16:30).

Further, Ecclesiastes 9:5 says; *"For the living know that they shall die: but the dead know not any thing, neither have they any more a reward; for the memory of them is forgotten. Also their love, and their hatred, and their envy, is now perished; neither have they any more a portion for ever in any thing that is done under the sun."*

The Pagans and Greeks also believed demons were the spirits of dead human heroes: But the Bible again states; *"And as it is appointed unto men once to die, but after this*

49

the judgment." (Hebrews 9:27). Finally to debunk the argument or analogy of demons being the spirita of the dead, Job 14 teaches that the dead exist in a realm separated from the current events on the earth.

So what are demons and what is their origin?

The word demon(s) does not appear in the King James Bible, which uses the word "devils" instead. The New King James Bible and some other new English translations use the word "demon(s)" in 72 verses and we must understand that they are not figments of man's imagination or myths and fictions of certain cultures and traditions.

THE ORIGIN OF DEMONS

God created angels before He created the heavens and the earth; but one-third of them became demons when they rebelled against God. Demons were angels; and everything that the Scriptures teach about the nature of angels - except for holiness - is true of demons. Demons are fallen angels, they are unholy angels; ones that have chosen to rebel against God and have retained their defiled, sinful nature since that time. A simple definition of demons is: an unholy, rebellious, corrupted and perverted angel bent on destroying the plans, the works, and the people of God; indeed, all people. The holy angels are referred to as an innumerable company in Hebrews 12:22; *"But ye are come unto mount Sion, and unto the city of the living God, the heavenly Jerusalem, and to an innumerable company of angels,"* and they are still innumerable even though they are only two-thirds of the original number of holy angels. When satan rebelled against God, one-third of the angels of God who sided with him were also cast down. *"And his tail drew the third part of the stars of heaven, and did cast them to the earth:... And there was war in heaven: Michael and his angels fought against the dragon; and the dragon fought and his angels, And prevailed not; neither was their place found any more in heaven. And the great dragon was cast out, that old serpent, called the Devil, and satan, which deceiveth the whole world: he was cast out into the earth, and his angels were cast out with him."* (Revelations 12:4, 7-9) This number is made up of all the different ranks or classes of angels; cherubim, seraphim, and the lowest rank of angels we simply refer to as angels.

Demons are fallen angels, they are unholy angels; ones that have chosen to rebel against God and have retained their defiled, sinful nature since that time.

Evil spirits or demons are not just influences; they are actual beings or personalities just like human beings. As I mentioned earlier, man is a tripartite being so though we are spirit, we have a body. Demons on the other hand do not have tangible physical existence so they desire to dwell in earthen vessels (human beings) in order to manifest themselves. Because their prime motive is to destroy everything that God does, they deploy wicked, malicious and simply appalling means to achieve this aim. And because of the love of God for the human race, they wish to hurt and destroy it. They start warfare with man once he becomes born again.

"For we wrestle not against flesh and blood, but against principalities, against powers, against the rulers of the darkness of this world, against spiritual wickedness in high places". (Ephesians 6:12)

Note that satan is not capable of creating his own forces because the Bible says that all things were created by God (Colossians 1:16). Satan is not an originator, he is an imitator and a perverter of everything that God does. This nature of impersonation is reflected even in the hierarchy of his kingdom.

The above scripture gives us insight about the structures and setup of satan's kingdom. Let us examine each one of them according to their order of rank and their varying degrees of authority as well as their functions.

PRINCIPALITIES

The word principality is derived from the Greek word "archias" meaning "rule" or government. These are princes of the dark kingdom who manipulate certain sections of the universe. They are ruling spirits assigned over nations, cities or territories.

Principalities are the highest rank in satan's kingdom and have been delegated the power to influence the affairs of nations and kingdoms contrary to God's original intent concerning their domain. They exert their influence through heads of states and kings and other natural rulers in the operational jurisdiction.

They instigate natural rulers to pass laws and decrees that contradict the laws of the almighty God and determine the livelihoods of the people that live within their jurisdiction.

Former Nazi ruler Adolf Hitler is a typical example of a human under the influence of these principalities in the natural realm. He is said to have exterminated about 6 million Jews in Nazi concentration camps.

Russia also came under the influence of principalities that worked through human vessels for about twenty-seven years through communist rule. This influence was extended over almost half of the nations of the world at the time and brought suffering and misery to the citizens of the nations under its influence.

In the Bible, as a result of praying and studying the scrolls, Daniel discovered a prophecy that had to do with the emancipation of him and his people from the kingdom of Persia. At the time he discovered this prophecy, he and his people had already served seventy years in captivity.

According to Jeremiah, God said He would send the Jews into captivity to allow their land to rest for a period of seventy years. But the appointed time and duration had long elapsed and there was still no sign of freedom for the Jews.

When Daniel prayed, he caused a stirring in the heavens and called God into remembrance of His word concerning Israel. God then decided it was time to bring His promise to pass, having found a vessel in the earth realm in the person of Daniel, an intercessor who stood in the gap and called upon God to intervene in the affairs of men and to do His will. An angel was then dispatched to respond to the prayers of Daniel but there was a satanic interference;

"Then said he unto me, Fear not, Daniel: for from the first day that thou didst set thine heart to understand, and to chasten thyself before thy God, thy words were heard, and I am come for thy words. But the prince of the kingdom of Persia withstood me one and twenty days: but, lo, Michael, one of the chief princes, came to help me; and I remained there with the kings of Persia. Now I am come to make thee understand what shall befall thy people in the latter days: for yet the vision is for many days. And when he had spoken such words unto me, I set my face toward the ground, and I became dumb. And, behold, one like the similitude of the sons of men touched my lips: then I opened my mouth, and spake, and said unto him that stood before me, O my lord, by the vision my sorrows are turned upon me, and I have retained no strength. For how can the servant of this my lord talk with this my lord? for as for me, straightway there remained no strength in me, neither is there breath left in me. Then there came again and touched me one like the appearance of a man, and he strengthened me, And said, O man greatly beloved, fear not: peace be unto thee, be strong, yea, be strong. And when he had spoken unto me, I

was strengthened, and said, Let my lord speak; for thou
hast strengthened me. Then said he, Knowest thou
wherefore I come unto thee? and now will I return to fight
with the prince of Persia: and when I am gone forth, lo, the
prince of Grecia shall come. But I will shew thee that which
is noted in the scripture of truth: and there is none that
holdeth with me in these things, but Michael your prince."
(Daniel 10:12-21)

The scripture reveals that from the first day Daniel
committed himself to fasting and prayer, God released an
answer. The angel was dispatched from the third heavens,
but to reach Daniel in the earth realm, he had to transit
through the second and the first heavens. He was, however,
opposed by a personality in the second heavens which he
referred to as the prince of Persia.

We see here that though there was only one kingdom of
Persia, there were two rulers. One ruled in the natural, in
the person of Darius and the other ruled in the spirit realm.
The unseen ruler governed the Kingdom of Persia behind
the scenes by his influence over the natural ruler.

POWERS

Powers are the second level of authority in satan's
kingdom. They exert their influence on decision making
bodies of nations, causing structures of governing
authorities to promote wickedness by controlling law
makers and people in places of authority.

Again, in reference to Daniel, we see how the governors and counselors conspired against Daniel and convinced king Darius to issue a decree banning all religious activity, all in an attempt to eliminate Daniel.

"Then this Daniel was preferred above the presidents and princes, because an excellent spirit was in him; and the king thought to set him over the whole realm. Then the presidents and princes sought to find occasion against Daniel concerning the kingdom; but they could find none occasion nor fault; forasmuch as he was faithful, neither was there any error or fault found in him. Then said these men, We shall not find any occasion against this Daniel, except we find it against him concerning the law of his God. Then these presidents and princes assembled together to the king, and said thus unto him, King Darius, live for ever. All the presidents of the kingdom, the governors, and the princes, the counsellors, and the captains, have consulted together to establish a royal statute, and to make a firm decree, that whosoever shall ask a petition of any God or man for thirty days, save of thee, O king, he shall be cast into the den of lions. Now, O king, establish the decree, and sign the writing, that it be not changed, according to the law of the Medes and Persians, which altereth not. Wherefore king Darius signed the writing and the decree." (Daniel 6:3-9)

Although Daniel was the only righteous man in the government--though he stood alone, he still posed a threat to the enemy; hence, they sought to destroy him.

Powers influence the thoughts and feelings of human beings. They can lead people to commit murder, steal and indulge in all kinds of destructive behavior and can even cause Christians to have a lackadaisical attitude towards the work of God and convince them to give more attention to other issues of less relevance in to their lives. Powers also influence Christians against doing anything that will better their Christian lives, like paying tithes and being in constant fellowship with God through fasting and prayer and the study of the word.

One of the major assignments of these powers is also to bring disunity amongst Christians and church leaders even within the same church. They stir up strife and contentions amongst members and leadership just to ensure that the work of God does not advance.

They have the ability to influence thoughts and emotions of human beings and even influence Christians for destructive purposes if they are not firmly grounded.

RULERS OF DARKNESS

The original word used in Greek to describe rulers of darkness is "kosmokrateros", which means "world rulers." They are mandated by the devil to promote false religions and occult practices, thereby enslaving the souls of men by deception. Kings and rulers enforce false religions on their people under the influence and workings of these rulers of darkness.

In some nations and kingdoms, it is a crime to be a Christian and the penalty for that so called crime is death. For instance, an entire nation has the Quran as their constitution and Islamic law is strictly enforced.

The goal of these rulers of darkness is to control. They deceive humans and feed their minds with false teachings, visions and dreams. They promote astrology, humanism, divination, witchcraft and other false religions simply to deceive people and turn them against the will of God.

SPIRITUAL HOST OF WICKEDNESS

Spiritual host of wickedness are responsible for promoting lawlessness and wickedness as the name clearly depicts. They use spiritual influence to ensnare man into all kinds of sin like homosexuality, rape, drug addiction, murder and every other social vice that is known to man.

They are very difficult to identify but the key to their operations is in the name – wickedness. Witchcraft and water spirits fall under this rank of satan's kingdom. Spiritual wickedness is responsible for accidents, premature death, and everything that seeks to hurt any member of the human race. They even orchestrate and devise ways to hinder and frustrate the people of God in order to fight their faith.

They may even appear as angels of light to lure Christians into destruction.

They even try to interfere with sermons and messages from the pulpit, cause disorder or distraction in the church, cast spells on people to sleep during church services just to deprive them from the benefits of the word of God and also convince the unsaved that it is well with them.

The existence of evil spirits is not imaginary, they are real beings that we have to acknowledge and deal with accordingly. The Apostles believed and spoke of the existence of demons in the New Testament. Matthew spoke of their end; *"Then shall he say also unto them on the left hand, Depart from me, ye cursed, into everlasting fire, prepared for the devil and his angels":* (Matthew 25:41). See the phrase "the devil and his angels"? Luke also gave extensive revelations about their nature, expulsion and their dwelling place. Concerning their nature he revealed; *"And in the synagogue there was a man, which had a spirit of an unclean devil, and cried out with a loud voice,"* (Luke 4:33). He also reveals; *"And they that were vexed with unclean spirits..."* (Luke 6:18). In Luke 9, he writes of their expulsion from human beings; *"And as he was yet a coming, the devil threw him down, and tare him. And Jesus rebuked the unclean spirit, and healed the child, and delivered him again to his father."* (Luke 9:42) And concerning their dwelling place, Luke writes the following;

"And when he went forth to land, there met him out of the city a certain man, which had devils long time, and ware no clothes, neither abode in any house, but in the tombs. When he saw Jesus, he cried out, and fell down before him, and

with a loud voice said, What have I to do with thee, Jesus, thou Son of God most high? I beseech thee, torment me not. (For he had commanded the unclean spirit to come out of the man. For oftentimes it had caught him: and he was kept bound with chains and in fetters; and he brake the bands, and was driven of the devil into the wilderness.) And Jesus asked him, saying, What is thy name? And he said, Legion: because many devils were entered into him. And they besought him that he would not command them to go out into the deep. And there was there an herd of many swine feeding on the mountain: and they besought him that he would suffer them to enter into them. And he suffered them. Then went the devils out of the man, and entered into the swine: and the herd ran violently down a steep place into the lake, and were choked". (Luke 8:27-33).

These verses even allowed Luke to further reveal that these demons operate just like human beings, and that they have their own identity. Apostle Paul also bears witness of their existence when he writes to Timothy and warns him of the doctrine of devils; *"Now the Spirit speaketh expressly, that in the latter times some shall depart from the faith, giving heed to seducing spirits, and doctrines of devils"* (1Timothy 4:1). More light is shed on the subject of the existence of these demons and their assignment in Revelations 16:14; *"For they are the spirits of devils, working miracles, which go forth unto the kings of the earth and of the whole world, to gather them to the battle of that great day of God Almighty."* Even the Lord Jesus acknowledged their existence; *"And he said to her, for this statement you may go your way; the demon has left your daughter."* (Mark 7:29 ESV).

We can then establish that evil spirits or demons, do exist and they operate within the earth even though they are unseen.

The names and titles of demons clearly depict their specific mission, assignment and areas of influence, manipulation and even in some cases possession and control. For instance, Matthew 12 speaks of a blind spirit or spirit of blindness; *"Then was brought unto him one possessed with a devil, blind, and dumb: and he healed him, insomuch that the blind and dumb both spake and saw."* (Matthew 12:22). There is also a "deaf and dumb spirit"; *"When Jesus saw that the people came running together, he rebuked the foul spirit, saying unto him, Thou dumb and deaf spirit, I charge thee, come out of him, and enter no more into him."* (Mark 9:25) and spirit of infirmity; *"And, behold, there was a woman which had a spirit of infirmity eighteen years, and was bowed together, and could in no wise lift up herself."* (Luke 13:11). Other names given to these evil spirits are "spirit of seduction"; (1 Timothy 4:1), "spirit of jealousy"; *"This is the law of jealousies, when a wife goeth aside to another instead of her husband, and is defiled; Or when the spirit of jealousy cometh upon him, and he be jealous over his wife, and shall set the woman before the Lord, and the priest shall execute upon her all this law."* (Numbers 5:29-30). And there are also "familiar spirits" *"A man also or woman that hath a familiar spirit,*

61

*or that is a wizard, shall surely be put to death: they shall
stone them with stones: their blood shall be upon them."*
(Leviticus 20:27).

CHARACTERISTICS OF DEMONS

Demons possess certain attributes and characteristics just
like humans. In Matthew 12, the demon who went out of a
man says, it will return," showing they have their own will.
*"Then he saith, I will return into my house from whence I
came out; and when he is come, he findeth it empty, swept,
and garnished."* (Matthew 12:44). The demon here
exercises its will to make a decision, and then follows it up
with the corresponding action. The verse that follows also
indicates that demons can be united to fulfil the same goal.
*"Then goeth he, and taketh with himself seven other spirits
more wicked than himself, and they enter in and dwell
there: and the last state of that man is worse than the first.
Even so shall it be also unto this wicked generation."*
(Matthew 12:45). Jesus had earlier spoken of the unity of
demons; *"And if Satan cast out Satan, he is divided against
himself; how shall then his kingdom stand?"* (Matthew
12:26). Jesus reveals that the kingdom of satan is able to
stand because it is not divided against itself, all the workers
of satan's kingdom have one agenda and that is to oppose
and destroy good. This revelation is key because, one of the
ways satan's kingdom fights the church is to incite personal
ambitions and cause Christians not to be united, by doing
so, satan's forces gain an advantage.

The Bible reveals that demons have emotions. *"Thou believest that there is one God; thou doest well: the devils also believe, and tremble"* (James 2:19). Trembling is an outward mark of strong emotion. Derek Prince writes that at times he has seen a demonized person, who when confronted with the authority of Christ, began to tremble violently and I have on many occasions dealt with and cast out devils, who pleaded for mercy and cried and trembled with fear. It is interesting to know that these demons know and obey the authority of Jesus Christ, for which reason they express fear at the mention of His name. They know the identity of Jesus Christ and would not dare to disobey Him or the mention of His name.

Demons also have intellect. They have knowledge not derived from natural sources, rather evil sources. The first time Jesus confronted a demonized man in the synagogue in Capernaum, the demon spoke out of the man; *"And there was in their synagogue a man with an unclean spirit; and he cried out, Saying, Let us alone; what have we to do with thee, thou Jesus of Nazareth? art thou come to destroy us? I know thee who thou art, the Holy One of God."* (Mark 1:23-24) It was more than a year before Jesus' own disciples began to realize what this demon had discerned immediately. This Scripture reiterates the fact that Jesus Christ has authority over all demons and they know and they respect it.

When Jesus asked the demonized man in the country of the Gadarenes in Mark 5:9, "What is your name?" a demon answered on behalf of itself and the other demons, "My name is Legion; for we are many." It shows that demons have self-awareness. The demon was aware of both its own identity and that of the other demons occupying this man. It also establishes the fact that they have names.

Demons can also speak. In the first three gospels and also in Acts, we see several examples of demons able to speak through the vocal organs of the people they are occupying. The demons could and still do answer questions and carry on a conversation. Normally, we regard the ability to speak as a distinctive mark of personality. They even lie; *"Ye are of your father the devil, and the lusts of your father ye will do. He was a murderer from the beginning, and abode not in the truth, because there is no truth in him. When he speaketh a lie, he speaketh of his own: for he is a liar, and the father of it."* (John 8:44). They are sometimes even referred to as "lying spirits."

Demons display a wide range of character traits. Some are vicious, violent and supernaturally strong. Others are weak and even ridiculous - characteristics one would not expect to find in a demon, or a spirit being for that matter.

UNSEEN FORCES AT WORK

Demons desire to express themselves through a physical body, they are not happy unless they occupy or possess a human body and in cases where they cannot find human bodies to fulfill their active needs, they will settle for the body of an animal. We see an example of this when Jesus cast out demons from a man. *"So the devils besought him, saying, If thou cast us out, suffer us to go away into the herd of swine. And he said unto them, Go. And when they were come out, they went into the herd of swine: and, behold, the whole herd of swine ran violently down a steep place into the sea, and perished in the waters."* (Matthew 8:31-32).

Just like the name of a person tells you who they are and their works, attitude, behaviors, tell you what they are made of, we can recognize what demonic power is at work in a person by what that person manifests. For instance, a very quick tempered person may be dealing with a "demon of anger." A woman who is barren would likely be dealing with a "demon of barrenness." And a person who is unable to keep a stable relationship or a job could be dealing with a "demon of instability."

There is also proof that evil spirits or demons cause diseases and sickness in human beings. There are several cases of medical conditions which doctor's science cannot explain. Job is an example in the Bible of inexplicable causes of sickness. Satan caused sores to appear on Job's body and no medicine could heal him. Job had no disability or sickness and nothing could explain the appearance of boils and sores on his body. It was purely the work of the devil. *"So went Satan forth from the presence of the Lord, and smote Job with sore boils from the sole of his foot unto his crown."* (Job 2:7). And for Job to be healed, God had to step in and deliver him.

There are also cases of deafness and dumbness that are caused by demons. *"As they went out, behold, they brought to him a dumb man possessed with a devil. And when the devil was cast out, the dumb spake: and the multitudes marvelled, saying, It was never so seen in Israel."* (Matthew 9:32-33).

Demons cause insanity and epilepsy and in some cases can make people manifest strength beyond natural capacity. An example is shown in the Bible when a man was able to break chains that were used to bind him. *"Who had his dwelling among the tombs; and no man could bind him, no, not with chains: Because that he had been often bound with fetters and chains, and the chains had been plucked asunder by him, and the fetters broken in pieces: neither could any man tame him."* (Mark 5:3-4). One of my spiritual son's was one day taking a young girl through deliverance from the spirit of insanity. The young girl was about seventeen years old and rather smallish for her age. She must have weighed about sixty to seventy pounds. This son was well built, about six feet and five inches tall and weighed about 200 pounds. While casting out the demon, a physical struggle ensued between him and the young girl who was now manifesting the demon physically. With both hands, the young girl somehow managed to lift the man who was more than two times her weight and attempted to slam him to the ground. In a very natural situation, this young girl could not have been able to lift anything above her own body weight, but with the workings of an unseen force, she exhibited supernatural strength.

Remember the story in the Bible of the seven men who attempted to cast out a devil? *"Then certain of the vagabond Jews, exorcists, took upon them to call over them which had evil spirits the name of the Lord Jesus, saying, We adjure you by Jesus whom Paul preacheth. And there were seven sons of one Sceva, a Jew, and chief of the priests, which did so. And the evil spirit answered and said, Jesus I know, and Paul I know; but who are ye? And the man in whom the evil spirit was leaped on them, and overcame them, and prevailed against them, so that they fled out of that house naked and wounded."* (Acts 19:13-16) One man possessed with an evil spirit overpowered nine men, stripped off their clothes and wounded them. This is not possible in the natural but a man possessed with a demon can manifest the strength of that demon.

According to Romans 8:15, demons cause bondage; *"For ye have not received the spirit of bondage again to fear; but ye have received the Spirit of adoption, whereby we cry, Abba, Father."* And they can also cause oppression; *"How God anointed Jesus of Nazareth with the Holy Ghost and with power: who went about doing good, and healing all that were oppressed of the devil; for God was with him."* (Acts 10:38)

Dr. Lester Sumrall wrote; "John, Jesus' beloved friend, a disciple, clearly defined for us what satan and his hosts are doing. In so doing, John portrayed Jesus in the shepherd function, and the devil as a thief. It is an easily understood parable.

"The thief cometh not, but for to steal, and to kill, and to destroy: I am come that they might have life, and that they might have it more abundantly." (John 10:10).

The devil steals health and sanity, he kills by cancer and other devouring diseases and the devil destroys spirit, soul and body of any human who yields to his deceptions.

Apart from demons affecting individual lives, they also attack broader areas of human life/society. In my book entitled *Binding the Strong Man,* I mentioned some of these areas and explained how demonic forces (strong men) attempt to capture and control society. However, I would use this book to reflect on these once more.

NATIONS, CITIES AND TERRITORIES

Satan's work through his demons can dominate and influence entire societies, morally, spiritually, politically, and economically. In modern history, the influence of men like Adolf Hitler and Mussolini shook society and even an entire race. Under the influence of satan, they made boastful statements. Mussolini even said, "I would shake hands with the devil if he helped me get the desires of my heart."

Satan seeks to capture empires and nations and to dominate them. The Bible speaks of Babylon and how it gave itself to sorceries, witchcraft and the occult. In the natural, Babylon was a great city that boasted of hanging gardens and other intriguing sights but it was also a city dominated by evil. An evil spirit, a principality for that matter, which attempted to keep Daniel's prayers from being answered when he dwelt there. (Daniel 10:20-21)

Sodom and Gomorrah are also examples in the Bible of cities that came under a peculiar demonic influence and domination. The spirit that ruled there caused men to sleep with men rather than with women. This sin of sodomy dominated an entire city so much that God had to wipe them out. There were under the influence of satan and his demons that were assigned to cause men to commit this particular type of sin. These spirits resist the purpose of God for whatever jurisdiction they operate in and do all they can to enforce satan's will for it. They are referred to as territorial spirits and this is why certain nations or locations are gripped with specific moral or social issues. In such instances, only the persistent prayers and fasting of intercessors can bring intervention to these places.

This sin of sodomy dominated an entire city so much that God had to wipe them out. There were under the influence of satan and his demons that were assigned to cause men to commit this particular type of sin. These spirits resist the purpose of God for whatever jurisdiction they operate in.

Today, there are cities and even nations that have been dominated by peculiar situations and challenges and this is a result of the work of satan and his demons.

CULTURE, RELIGION AND BELIEFS

Territorial spirits can also dominate places in the areas of religion. They impose a particular religion over a nation or a city and inspire leaders to create laws through such religion to oppose the will of God. The "Sharia law" of Islam is one of such demonic laws that the enemy uses in cities to fight God's people. In places in the northern parts of Nigeria where this law operates, people are put to death for believing or having faith in any other religion.

In other societies, witchcraft, satanism, occultism and traditional worship have completely blinded the minds and the hearts of people so that they practice these beliefs and perform many rituals to their own hurt. Ritual murders are committed and animal and human sacrifices are made in the name of some of these false religions and beliefs. Their rituals are performed to acquire wealth or gain supernatural protection amongst other reasons.

FAMILIES

There are certain trends and traits that can be identified in members of a particular family for many generations. Certain negative cycles may occur one generation after the other. These reflect the influence and control of a particular spirit.

In some families, anyone who tries to excel in life dies prematurely. In other families, women do not marry, and if they do they soon get divorced. These are limitations that satan and his demons set over families to oppose God's plan for their lives. These limitations operate in the form of curses. In some cases, it might be a particular sickness or disease which medicine will refer to as "hereditary." But as Christians, "we are not ignorant of his devices." Most common negative trends that run through a family from one generation to the other are the work of demons.

There are many operations of different spirits, which must be identified in order to set the captives of such spirits free. In identifying these demons, we must investigate the prevalent lifestyle of a person, or place, the culture and traditions that dominate a geographic area and the extent of the spread of the gospel and persistent challenges.

DEMONIC ACCESS

Satan operates through legalities and technicalities. Before he and his demons take over a person or a territory, they seek for an occasion, an opening that gives them access to do as they please. When David sinned against God, God forgave him but said to him that he had given the enemy an occasion. *"Howbeit, because by this deed thou hast given great occasion to the enemies of the Lord to blaspheme, the child also that is born unto thee shall surely die."* (2 Samuel 12:14).

These occasions and doorways are what give demons the right to enter into lives and the grounds upon which to stay. Evil hates everything that is good so satan and his agents will not stop making attempts to exact on humans. Where they do not find legal grounds, they will stir up situations to gain one.

These occasions and doorways are what give demons the right to enter into lives and the grounds upon which to stay. Where they do not find legal grounds, they will stir up situations to gain one.

A text in the Isaiah depicts such operations of the enemy. *"Let us go up against Judah, and vex it, and let us make a breach therein for us, and set a king in the midst of it, even the son of Tabeal:"* (Isaiah 7:6). By this scripture, we see clearly how the enemy works. First, they stir up situations to vex their target and once the target yields to their vexation or temptation, a breach is created. This breach becomes the door way and the spiritual legal grounds upon which the enemy will stand to assign a demon to the life of a person. Kings rule, therefore we understand that by the workings of that demon who is now a king in the life of the target, the actions and inactions and even situations around the life of the target will be influenced or controlled by the demon.

Satan and his demons use many grounds and doorways to access and dominate human lives, I shall explain some of these doorways.

SINFUL ACTS AND HABITS

Sin is the number one doorway for the demons to enter and to dominate human lives. When one sins an opening is created which gives demons the legal grounds to enter even the lives of believers. The sin that one commits and the demon that enters the life of the person as a result of the sin is usually alike in nature. When one commits the sin of fornication, he or she becomes vulnerable to the demon of lust or fornication.

MEDIA

The media in recent times has become a major doorway for demons to dominate and influence human lives. Certain films, books, newspapers, magazines and television can give demons very quick and easy access to the lives of people. When people watch or read pornographic material, a demon of fornication, adultery or sexual lust can access them. Horror movies and materials of violent nature can also introduce demons of fear and even murder into the lives of people.

CIRCUMSTANCES AND SITUATIONS

We encounter situations and circumstances for which we are not prepared in life. The enemy can use these moments and instances to gain access and dominate the lives of individuals. In moments of weakness, whether physical, emotional or spiritual, people unconsciously lose their ability to resist satan and his demons. For example, in moments of sickness, an individual can be afraid, anxious or deeply troubled. In such a state, resistance against evil is very low and a demon can easily gain access.

When a woman has dated a man for a long time and they plan to get married, set a date and make all the necessary preparations, then suddenly the man abandons her, she may become very disappointed, hence open the door to a spirit of disappointment and rejection.

A spirit of grief can also enter into the life of an individual if they lose a very close family member. In times of anger, envy and jealousy, a demon can move into the life of a person to carry out the will of satan. There are many circumstances by which the enemy may try to gain access to the lives of people. So, it is important to resist him always. The Bible says; *"Submit yourselves therefore to God. Resist the devil, and he will flee from you."* (James 4:7).

OCCULT AND IDOLATRY

Idolatry and occultism are of the same root. Idolatry is the worship of demons and anything other than God and occultism is the use of demonic powers for self-gain. Let us study the scripture below:

But were mingled among the heathen, and learned their works. And they served their idols: which were a snare unto them. Yea, they sacrificed their sons and their daughters unto devils, And shed innocent blood, even the blood of their sons and of their daughters, whom they sacrificed unto the idols of Canaan: and the land was polluted with blood. Thus were they defiled with their own works, and went a whoring with their own inventions. Therefore was the wrath of the Lord kindled against his people, insomuch that he abhorred his own inheritance. And he gave them into the hand of the heathen; and they that hated them ruled over them. Their enemies also oppressed them, and they were brought into subjection under their hand." (Psalm 106:35-42).

The scripture speaks of the consequences of idolatry because God has already instructed His people against worshiping other Gods. *"Thou shalt have none other gods before me. Thou shalt not make thee any graven image, or any likeness of any thing that is in heaven above, or that is in the earth beneath, or that is in the waters beneath the earth: Thou shalt not bow down thyself unto them, nor serve them: for I the Lord thy God am a jealous God, visiting the iniquity of the fathers upon the children unto the third and fourth generation of them that hate me,"* (Deuteronomy 5:7-9).

This is what occurs when people disobey God because of their cultural or traditional practices.

CURSES

A curse according to biblical definition is God's recompense in the life of man and his descendants as a result of iniquity. Curses can give the strong man access to an individual. A curse offers demons legal grounds to operate in people's lives. The danger about curses is that, they can affect born-again Christians. The fact that something is legally yours does not matter to the enemy. Satan and his demons work to deprive people of all that belong to them. They will seek out grounds to deny people of the will of God for their lives.

God's word teaches that we are healed by the stripes of Jesus; but it is our duty to appropriate the Word in order to for it to take effect in our lives. Otherwise, we cannot benefit from the blessing of divine healing. A believer cannot be legally under a curse—but can be under the influence of a curse until he or she is delivered.

Words are spirits. Whenever a word is spoken, the spirit of that word is released to ensure fulfillment of that word. When a word of blessing is spoken, the spirit of that word will ensure that the word comes to pass–irrespective of the time and duration. Therefore, blessings can be inherited from past generations.

In the same sense, when an evil word or curse is uttered, the spirit of that word will carry out the contents of that evil word or curse.

One can be cursed right from the womb and one can also be blessed from the womb. *"Thou shewest lovingkindness unto thousands, and recompensest the iniquity of the fathers into the bosom of their children after them: ..."* (Jeremiah 32:18).

Some individuals, because of a curse, are estranged from the womb; *"The wicked are estranged from the womb: they go astray as soon as they be born, speaking lies.*" (Psalm 58:3). So, children can be born with curses. Curses also give satan and his demons control over households and these demons cannot be bound and cast out unless the curses that gave them legal grounds are broken.

"They that see thee shall narrowly look upon thee, and consider thee, saying, Is this the man that made the earth to tremble, that did shake kingdoms; That made the world as a wilderness, and destroyed the cities thereof; that opened not the house of his prisoners? All the kings of the nations, even all of them, lie in glory, every one in his own house." (Isaiah 14:16-18).

There is no limit to what satan and his demons can destroy until we interrupt and stop his work in the name of Jesus. The Bible says, *"... For this purpose the Son of God was manifested, that he might destroy the works of the devil."* (1John 3:8).

Other doorways that give access to satan and his demons are uncleanness, seared conscience, immorality, demonic doctrines, sodomy, debauchery, whoredom, witchcraft and every other act that is considered as the a work of the flesh.

"Now the works of the flesh are manifest, which are these; Adultery, fornication, uncleanness, lasciviousness, Idolatry, witchcraft, hatred, variance, emulations, wrath, strife, seditions, heresies, Envyings, murders, drunkenness, revellings, and such like: of the which I tell you before, as I have also told you in time past, that they which do such

77

things shall not inherit the kingdom of God." (Galatians 5:19-21)

There certainly could be more than could listed here, but whenever you notice that any one of the above is in control of an individual, family, church community, or nation, you can be sure that a demon is in operation.

Jezebel

Jezebel is the strong man of idolatry, seduction, rebellion, and sexual sins. He/she is also the spirit that opposes spiritual authority in the church by inciting the people to spiritual harlotry.

This spirit loves to masquerade as a prophet of God to undermine the true prophets of God. When not identified, this spirit can bring much havoc into the church.

Jezebel is also a demon of witchcraft—both in the church and in domineering, abusive, manipulative, and exploitative persons. Such individuals will always seek to enforce their will and will not be subject to authority in a godly setup. Jezebel is a spirit who manifests his/her operations in both men and women.

In the book of Revelations, Jesus rebukes the church for allowing Jezebel to have her way and threatens to destroy her and her followers.

"Notwithstanding I have a few things against thee, because thou sufferest that woman Jezebel, which calleth herself a

prophetess, to teach and to seduce my servants to commit fornication, and to eat things sacrificed unto idols. And I gave her space to repent of her fornication; and she repented not. Behold, I will cast her into a bed, and them that commit adultery with her into great tribulation, except they repent of their deeds." (Revelations 2:20-22).

The spirit of Jezebel must be confronted and dealt with without any compromise. Again, in this case, it is the Word of God that is the sole weapon to defeat, bind, and paralyze this spirit.

CHAPTER FIVE

EXAMPLES OF SATANIC OPERATIONS: EXCERPTS FROM BINDING THE STRONG MAN

As I pointed out in chapter three of my book *Binding the Strongman*, demons do not operate in isolation, but with a host of other spirits. Some stronger, high-ranking demons have strongholds made up of lesser ranking demons that execute their orders.

The strategies employed by demons against man have one ultimate goal—to stop people, families, societies, and nations from fulfilling their dreams and God's plan for their lives. It is their aim to abort the purposes of God. When God created man, His aim for man was for fellowship between man and Himself. This was cut off in the Garden of Eden. However, God, in His abundant mercies, through Jesus Christ, has restored this fellowship.

Through the ages, satan sought to make the coming of Jesus impossible so that this fellowship would not be restored. He schemed and employed human beings, institutions, and establishments—knowingly or unknowingly—to pervert the course of justice and impose legislations contrary to the Word of God.

In this book, I have explained the hierarchies and chain of command within the satanic kingdom. In that chapter, we examined some of satan's operations through his command structure. Let us examine briefly, more examples from the Word of God. We shall look at the accounts of Moses, Esther, Jesus, Joseph, and David to see how satan employs legal and political systems against the people of God and also some attributes of some other spirits that characterize satan.

Moses

Before the birth of Moses, the people of Israel, then in Egypt because of Joseph, grew in all areas of their lives. A new king arose in Egypt who, according to the Scriptures, "knew not Joseph" (Exodus 1:8). Satan used this new king, a strong man, to oppress the Israelites. Satan, knowing that the deliverer of God's people was soon to appear, caused the new king to issue a decree to kill all newly born males among the Israelites:

"And he said, When ye do the office of a midwife to the Hebrew women, and see them upon the stools; if it be a son, then ye shall kill him: but if it be a daughter, then she shall live." (Exodus 1:16), and his aim was to abort the plan of God for the people of Israel, for them to remain in bondage; and he used legislation.

Today, satan is still in the same business. That is why legislations in many countries do not conform to the Word of God.

When satan's first plans failed, he caused the strong man of Egypt to issue another decree for all males born to Israelites to be thrown into the river Nile: *"And Pharaoh charged all his people, saying, Every son that is born ye shall cast into the river, and every daughter ye shall save alive."* (Exodus 1:22) It would be easy to deduce that the sons of Israel were to be used as sacrificial offerings to the gods of Egypt. All this happened to kill the deliverer of the nation of Israel. Please be aware that the enemy is fighting you, tooth and nail, to keep you from succeeding in life.

Satan is not omnipresent, and neither is he omnipotent. Otherwise, he would have pinpointed the specific family from which Moses was to be born; but he isn't, which is why he needs a network of agents to carry out his commands.

Jesus is all-knowing. If we have Jesus living inside of us, then greater is He who lives in us than he who is in the world: *"Ye are of God, little children, and have overcome them: because greater is he that is in you, than he that is in the world."* (1 John 4:4) By the help of the Holy Spirit, God has also made available to us revelation gifts—the gift of the word of knowledge and the gift of discerning of spirits, among them—with which we are able to detect the operations of the enemy. Friend, these gifts have been given to profit us. Let us desire them and walk in them. The apostle Paul said, "We are not ignorant of his [the devil's] devices." (2 Cor. 2:11)

Esther

The main focus of this account is how satan sought, through legislation, to exterminate the Jews. He employed the services of Haman, a strong man in the flesh. However, Mordecai got wind of the plan and helped Queen Esther to divert satan's purpose (Esther 3 through 5:14).

One operation of satan is to place his own people in strategic positions in a society so that they carry out his agenda. It is our duty as Christians to remove men and women who the enemy has planted in the corridors of power from their office, through prayer.

Jesus

When Jesus was born, the enemy orchestrated a plan to get rid of Him, knowing that Christ was to save mankind. Satan worked through Herod who was a schemer and a wicked ruler.

This is Herod's background: He was the son of Antipar, who wormed his way into the confidence of Julius Caesar. The Romans made him procurator of Judea. Later the descendant of the Maccabean dynasty, Antigonus, was executed. Herod craftily managed to stay in power despite the changing government of Rome. He was so evil that Caesar Augustus said, "I would rather be Herod's dog than his son."

Satan made full use of Herod to slaughter innocent infants in Bethlehem in an attempt to kill the Messiah. But God averted this by revealing to Joseph the enemy's plans. Joseph was sent to Egypt for the safekeeping of Jesus. As long as we stay in God's camp, He will reveal the strategies of our enemy.

Joseph and David

Satan and his demons sometimes operate through frame ups. Take Joseph's case as an example. The enemy employed Potiphar's wife to try to seduce Joseph into committing adultery. Joseph spurned her and fled, leaving his garment behind. Because she failed to get him to do what she wanted, she chose to frame Joseph, using his garment to accuse him of attempting to rape her:

"And it came to pass about this time, that Joseph went into the house to do his business; and there was none of the men of the house there within. And she caught him by his garment, saying, Lie with me: and he left his garment in her hand, and fled, and got him out. And it came to pass, when she saw that he had left his garment in her hand, and was fled forth, That she called unto the men of her house, and spake unto them, saying, See, he hath brought in an Hebrew unto us to mock us; he came in unto me to lie with me, and I cried with a loud voice: And it came to pass, when he heard that I lifted up my voice and cried, that he left his garment with me, and fled, and got him out. And she laid up his garment by her, until his lord came home. And she spake unto him according to these words, saying, The Hebrew servant, which thou hast brought unto us, came in unto me to mock me: And it came to pass, as I lifted up my

voice and cried, that he left his garment with me, and fled out. And it came to pass, when his master heard the words of his wife, which she spake unto him, saying, After this manner did thy servant to me; that his wrath was kindled. And Joseph's master took him, and put him into the prison, a place where the king's prisoners were bound: and he was there in the prison." (Genesis 39:11-20)

Who would not believe her? She was the wife of Potiphar, a respected member of the personal staff of Pharaoh, the king of Egypt. If Joseph had indeed committed this sin, who knows what would have become of his dreams? Child of God beware for satan is the accuser of the brethren.

Spirit beings without human bodies are able to influence humans who do not understand, to use the media—both electronic and print—to halt the purposes of God for individuals and for nations. Satan works against God's agents of change right in their corridors of power. He does it by discrediting them and thereby rendering them ineffective in bringing necessary change.

Satan uses people with all sorts of false allegations and half-truths to knowingly or unknowingly discredit individuals, organizations, churches, and men of God. His plan is to prevent the world from hearing them; even when they have a message of truth. Given these wrong perceptions, people turn to and prefer other leaders. This can cause vexation—leading a person into anger, even provoking such a person to self-destruction through wrong choices.

David committed sin by taking a census after he was provoked by the devil. Second Chronicles 21:1 says, *"And Satan stood up against Israel and provoked David to number Israel."*

Job

The story of Job is one that shows how the work of satan and his demons operate. It also reveals the truth about the existence of a "spirit realm" and the fact that it influences the natural realm:

"And the Lord said unto Satan, Behold, all that he hath is in thy power; only upon himself put not forth thine hand. So Satan went forth from the presence of the Lord. And there was a day when his sons and his daughters were eating and drinking wine in their eldest brother's house: And there came a messenger unto Job, and said, The oxen were plowing, and the asses feeding beside them: And the Sabeans fell upon them, and took them away; yea, they have slain the servants with the edge of the sword; and I only am escaped alone to tell thee. While he was yet speaking, there came also another, and said, The fire of God is fallen from heaven, and hath burned up the sheep, and the servants, and consumed them; and I only am escaped alone to tell thee. While he was yet speaking, there came also another, and said, The Chaldeans made out three bands, and fell upon the camels, and have carried them away, yea, and slain the servants with the edge of the sword; and I only am escaped alone to tell thee. While he was yet speaking, there came also another, and said, Thy

sons and thy daughters were eating and drinking wine in their eldest brother's house: And, behold, there came a great wind from the wilderness, and smote the four corners of the house, and it fell upon the young men, and they are dead; and I only am escaped alone to tell thee". (Job 1:12-19).

First of all, we must establish from verse 12 of this chapter of Job that it was satan who afflicted Job and not God. All that happened to Job was influenced and controlled by satan who is a spirit, though the events occurred in the natural.

The rest of the verses in the chapter reveal the mission of satan and his demons which was also confirmed by Jesus. That is to steal, to kill and to destroy:; "The thief cometh not, but for to steal, and to kill, and to destroy: *I am come that they might have life, and that they might have it more abundantly."* (John 10:10)

So we see how satan and his demons play a role in every negative thing that happens in the life of man. In verse 15, we see satan responsible for armed robbery and murder. In verse 16, we see him responsible for bankruptcy and fire outbreaks. Note that, all though the servant reported that; *"The fire of God is fallen from heaven, and hath burned up the sheep, and the servants, and consumed them;"* We have already established from verse 12 that God was not in any way involved in the acts and occurrences that afflicted the life of Job. Therefore, the fire was neither from God nor from His heaven but was from satan and his fire kingdom.

The words of the servant are important to note because this is the state of mind of the people of the world and even some believers. They think that all great disasters are from God but this scripture has taught us otherwise.

In verse 17 of the same chapter, we see satan at work again in the area of armed robbery, extortion and murder. Then one very remarkable event occurs in verse 19.

"And, behold, there came a great wind from the wilderness, and smote the four corners of the house, and it fell upon the young men, and they are dead; and I only am escaped alone to tell thee." (Job 1:19).

What most people refer to as a "natural disaster" or in some circles "an act of God." However, we see clearly from this verse that the wind that caused the natural disaster that resulted in the loss of the lives of the children of Job was from satan.

In Job 2, we see that satan and his demons are able to cause sickness. And they can also be the cause of tension and breakups in marriages and other relationships and other struggles and challenges in life.

"So went Satan forth from the presence of the Lord, and smote Job with sore boils from the sole of his foot unto his crown. And he took him a potsherd to scrape himself withal; and he sat down among the ashes. Then said his wife unto him, Dost thou still retain thine integrity? curse God, and die. But he said unto her, Thou speakest as one of the foolish women speaketh. What? shall we receive good

at the hand of God, and shall we not receive evil? In all this did not Job sin with his lips. " (Job 2:7-10)

It is therefore an undeniable fact that there are unseen powers at work in the lives of human beings.

God, by His grace and mercies, through the shed blood of our Lord Jesus, has given the believer authority over the strong man and I would like to emphasize the following points.

- If one wants to overcome satan and his demons, one must close all the doorways and deny them access.
- You must be born again. That means you must renounce sin in your life and receive Jesus Christ as your Lord and personal Savior. Believe and confess Him as your Lord (Romans 10:9-10).
- By prayer, claim the whole armor of God as your spiritual clothing.
- Claim victory by the blood of Jesus over the satan and his demons, and call upon the hosts of God to come against him.
- Use the Word of God, which is the sword of the Spirit, against them.
- Aggressively command demons to be cast out and bound in Jesus' name, and command whatever they have bound to be loosed.

CHAPTER SIX

AUTHORITY

OF THE

BELIEVER

SPIRITUAL WARFARE

Many believers ask why we must fight when Christ has already won the victory. Yes, Christ has already won the victory—but we [believers] have to *enforce* this victory and *superimpose* it over the enemy.

Many times when God spoke to Israel about their possessions and inheritance, He says He has given it to them but then commands them to possess it. *"Rise up, take your journey, ... behold, I have given into thine hand Sihon the Amorite, King of Hesbon, and his land: begin to possess it, and contend with him in battle."* (Deuteronomy 2:24)

God states clearly that He has given the Land to the children of Israel but He adds that they must contend with the current occupants of the land in order to possess it. We must go into spiritual warfare knowing that we are already victorious and the outcome shall not disfavor us. If we had to win the victory all by ourselves, we could never do it. Jesus has already won the victory for us; but it is time for us to enforce it and pick up the prize.

It is clear to us that Jesus has obtained all authority in heaven and on the earth and the only way the world can fully understand and appreciate this is for us to exercise His authority as we are commanded to:

"And Jesus came and spake unto them, saying, All power is given unto me in heaven and in earth. Go ye therefore, and teach all nations, baptizing them in the name of the Father, and of the Son, and of the Holy Ghost: Teaching them to observe all things whatsoever I have commanded you: and, lo, I am with you alway, even unto the end of the world. Amen." (Matthew 28:18-20)

The word "authority" is translated from a Greek word that means the right to use power. It also means the right to have one's words and commands obeyed.

The policeman is empowered by the government to enforce the law and to deal with lawbreakers. He has the power to arrest and detain those who disobey the law. When a judge declares someone guilty and passes out a sentence, it is the duty of the law enforcement agent to see to it that this sentence is executed.

This is exactly how the believer stands in Christ. We are mandated to *enforce* the laws and promises of our God over the spiritual lawbreakers, who sometimes carry out their activities through human agents. Even though a police officer may be physically feeble, his or her authority is not undermined; he is able to bring even a trailer to a stop by simply indicating with his hand. He has something more powerful than the power of the trailer's engine or tires. He has authority. He only has to lift his hand to signal stop, and the trailer comes to a halt.

We are mandated to enforce the laws and promises of our God over the spiritual lawbreakers, who sometimes carry out their activities through human agents.

The believer has the power of attorney to use the name of Jesus to bring the devices of the enemy to a halt. This example of the police officer illustrates that the extent to which you utilize your God-given authority will determine how far the enemy can advance in your life.

The Scripture says, *"Behold I give you authority to tread on serpents and scorpions and over all the power of the enemy: and nothing shall by any means hurt you"* (Luke 10:19).

Friend, you and I have been authorized by heaven as God's ambassadors to carry out and enforce the laws of Jehovah. We have the backing of the powers of heaven in this assignment. Just as the police officer is fully backed by the government of his nation, the believer has heavenly backing. The Scriptures say, *"Let the saints be joyful in glory: let them sing aloud upon their beds. Let the high praises of God be in their mouth, and a two-.edged sword in their hand; To execute vengeance upon the heathen, and punishments upon the people; To bind their kings with chains, and their nobles with fetters of iron; To execute upon them the judgment written: this honour have all his saints. Praise ye the Lord."* (Psalm 149:5-9).

Just as it is dangerous to defy the laws of the state, so is it dangerous for the enemy to defy the commands of the believer. Whenever the policeman takes off his uniform and cap, which are symbols of his authority and by which he is recognized and respected, he loses the authority. The believers who rebel against the laws of the kingdom of God lose their right and mandate to exercise authority over the devil (2 Cor. 10:3-6).

Just as it is dangerous to defy the laws of the state, so is it dangerous for the enemy to defy the commands of the believer.

IMPROPER DRESSING

God has provided a type of uniform for His saints to put on—you must make sure you have yours. You must be properly dressed.

The Christian life is a life full of battles. We have to be prepared as soldiers of the Lord at all times to wage spiritual warfare. The only way we can successfully do this is to put on the whole armor of God. We cannot let down our guard.

Can you imagine a soldier without his boots or helmet in battle? How about a soldier without his belt or a soldier dressed without his sword or gun? Yet, most believers are not properly dressed spiritually: many choose to select the pieces of armor that appeal to them and ignore the rest. This makes them vulnerable to the attacks of the enemy because the enemy takes advantage of their uncovered or unprotected areas.

The tendency for many Christians to dwell on just one part of the armor, such as faith, is dangerous. Each piece of the armor has its specific role, and one cannot be substituted for the other. Child of God, always remember that the armor is of God, and not of man (Ephesians 6:10-19).

Before I proceed, I want to stress and remind you that in dealing with the strong man, you are not dealing with only one entity, but rather with a host of demons which are under the command of the chief entity—satan. Therefore, victory over the strong man means overrunning the strongholds as well. In view of this, one must be totally equipped to be successful.

The tendency for many Christians to dwell on just one part of the armor, such as faith, is dangerous. Each piece of the armor has its specific role, and one cannot be substituted for the other.

THE WHOLE ARMOR OF GOD

"Wherefore take unto you the whole armour of God, that ye may be able to withstand in the evil day, and having done all, to stand. Stand therefore, having your loins girt about with truth, and having on the breastplate of righteousness; And your feet shod with the preparation of the gospel of peace; Above all, taking the shield of faith, wherewith ye shall be able to quench all the fiery darts of the wicked. And take the helmet of salvation, and the sword of the Spirit, which is the word of God: Praying always with all prayer and supplication in the Spirit, and watching thereunto with all perseverance and supplication for all saints;" (Ephesians 6:13-18)

God has not left us at the mercy of the enemy but has equipped us with weapons to walk in total victory every day in our Christian lives. The above Scripture opens God's armory to us. In the binding of the strong man, every believer will do well to make use of these weapons. Note there are two categories—the defensive and the offensive weapons. We shall examine each piece of the armor.

Always remember that "… *though we walk in the flesh, we do not war after the flesh: For the weapons of our warfare are not carnal, but mighty through God to the pulling down of strongholds; casting down imaginations, and every high thing that exalteth itself against the knowledge of God, and bringing into captivity every thought to the obedience of Christ; and having in a readiness to revenge all*

95

disobedience, when your obedience is fulfilled." (2 Corinthians 10:3-6)

DEFENSIVE WEAPONS

Belt of Truth

Our first weapon of defense is truth. To walk in truth is to oppose all manner of falsehood. To walk in truth is to walk in fidelity with the Word of God. To put on the belt of truth is to walk in integrity of heart, sincerity, transparency, and openness to God, to yourself, and to others. It means the absence of pretense, insincerity and hypocrisy.

To explain the uses of the belt of truth we must examine the physical uses of a natural belt. The belt goes around the middle part of our bodies to ensure that our clothes stay on.

"The wicked flee when no one pursues. But the righteous are bold as a lion" (Proverbs 28:1). Walking in truth is the basis of our boldness. Absence of boldness is fearfulness. A fearful man is a loser before he starts anything.

This explains why Gideon was asked to send back home all those who were of a fearful heart. *"Now therefore, proclaim in the ears of the people, saying, 'Whosoever is fearful and afraid, let him turn and depart at once from Mount Gilead.' So twenty-two thousand men left, while ten thousand remained."* (Judges 7:3)

Moses, the man of God, was also instructed to give similar warnings to the Israelites whenever they were ready for war. *"The officers shall say speak further to the people and say, 'What man is there who is fearful and faint-hearted? Let him go and return to his house, lest the heart of his brethren faint like his heart.'"* (Deuteronomy 20:8)

Another reason why the belt of truth must be in place is because the Bible says that satan, the accuser of the brethren, accuses us day and night before our God (Revelations 12:10). On the other hand, we overcome satan by the blood of the Lamb and the word of our testimony (Revelations 12:11). Two things are required that we must employ to defeat the accusations of satan—the blood of Jesus and the word of our testimony.

Breastplate of Righteousness

"And he [Abraham] believed in the LORD, and He accounted it to him for righteousness" (Genesis 15:6). Righteousness means to have a right standing with God. It has to do with our relationship with God. Righteousness cannot be earned by our work. Righteousness is higher than good works. It is imputed unto us as Christians when we become born again. That means, that to put on the breastplate of righteousness, I have to make sure that I walk in the righteousness of God and not in my own righteousness. Isaiah explains this better: *"But we are all like an unclean thing. And all our righteousnesses are like filthy rags "* (Isaiah 64:6).

Even though the Lord has clothed us with His righteousness, it is our responsibility to keep it on by living lives compatible to His Word. It means to walk a walk of cleanliness and to guard our hearts against any corruption.

"Keep your heart with diligence for out of it springs the issues of life" (Proverbs 4:23). The breastplate covers the chest. Underneath the chest is one of man's most vital organs, the heart. Our hearts influence our affections, and our affections influence everything else in our lives. It is amazing when you begin to ponder why God placed the heart of man in his chest. Man's heart is protected by ribs and when we put on the breastplate of righteousness, we protect our heart and all that has to do with it.

Feet Shod with the Preparation of the Gospel of Peace

A soldier must always be prepared for battle. He has to be instant in season and out of season. You cannot bind the strong man and overrun his stronghold when you are not prepared for battle.

To shod your feet with the gospel of peace is to wear shoes that are able to speed you on as you preach the Good News. It means we have to be ready and eager to preach or share the gospel always. It means we have to put on our boots for battle.

The soldier puts on boots by for two reasons. First, they help the soldier to stand firm. They keep him from slipping and sliding on difficult terrain. Sharing the gospel solidifies and stabilizes you in faith. Believers have a responsibility to study the Word of God, so that we can share it in confidence to have stability at all times. Second, boots increase one's mobility. They enable one to move quickly and fearlessly over rough or unfamiliar ground.

"How beautiful upon the mountains are the feet of him who brings good news, who proclaims peace, who brings good tidings, who proclaims salvation, who says to Zion, 'Your God reigns.'" (Isaiah 52:7).

The weapons of our warfare must be used in unison. For example, prayer alone cannot save your family members from the control of the enemy. Prayer has to be used with of the Word of God. The Word of God, which is the gospel of peace, must be used alongside prayer.

The Shield of Faith

"Above all, taking the shield of faith with which you will be able to quench the fiery darts of the wicked one." (Ephesians 6:16)

There are many definitions of faith, but the faith that is spoken of in the above scripture refers to unreserved confidence in God, absolute dependence on the integrity of God's Word, and complete reliance on the goodness of God. Faith is an unquestioning belief in God. *"But without faith it is impossible to please Him, for he who comes to God must believe that He is, and that He is a rewarder of those who diligently seek Him."* (Hebrews 11:6)

The shield of faith, the Scripture says, will enable you to "quench the fiery darts of the wicked one." Those fiery darts are flame-tipped arrows, and there is usually a barrage of them that is released before a main assault. They are sent out by satan to weaken your resolve and faith in God so that he can overpower you.

Fiery darts represent fierce, sudden, and unexpected attacks from the enemy. The enemy will want you to question God's Word and promises by drawing your attention to things that seemingly are not going right. But, lift up your shield of faith and protect yourself and then get ready to assault the strong man and completely overrun the stronghold while maintaining your stand.

"So then faith cometh by hearing, and hearing by the word of God." (Rom. 10:17) One of the assignments of the Holy Spirit in a believer's life is to put the believer in remembrance of the Word of God. Therefore, the more of the Word you have in you, the more the Holy Spirit will remind you of the Word in any particular situation. Conversely, if you do not study the Word, the Holy Spirit cannot remind you of the truth. Know that God has a word for every occasion.

"Let us who live in the light keep sober, protected by the armor of faith and love, and wearing as our helmet, the happy hope of salvation... Cling tightly to your faith in Christ and always keep your conscience clear, doing what you know is right... Let us draw near to God with a true heart in full assurance of faith, because we have been sprinkled with Christ's blood to make us clean, because our bodies have been washed with pure water... Fight the good

fight of faith."(1 Thess. 5:8; 1 Tim. 1:19; Heb. 10:22; 1 Tim. 6:12)

Helmet of Salvation

The head is one of the most important parts of our bodies; and in God's design, it is encased in a protective skull. It is common to hear about heart transplants, about kidney transplants, and about other limbs of the body being transplanted. However, we never hear about a head transplant or brain transplant.

"For as he thinks in his heart, so is he" (Prov. 23:7). What controls your mind controls your life. If you think defeat, you walk in defeat. If you think sickness, you walk in sickness. The enemy will constantly bombard your mind with all manner of thoughts that will cripple your walk with God.

The helmet is designed to protect the head. It is designed to protect our minds and our whole attitude toward our Christian faith. If the enemy fails in damaging us in other ways, he will try to make us weary, discouraged, and disillusioned with evil thoughts and imaginations.

"For the weapons of our warfare are not carnal but mighty through God for the pulling down of strongholds, casting down imaginations and every high thing that exalts itself against the knowledge of God, and bringing every thought into captivity to the obedience of Christ. And having in a readiness to revenge all disobedience, when your obedience is fulfilled" (2 Cor. 10:4).

To put on the helmet of salvation is to consistently read, study, and meditate on the Word of God. Meditation is to ponder, mutter, and reflect on the word. It is not to make one's mind blank, as is taught by eastern religions. This eastern religious method opens your mind to demonic control.

OFFENSIVE WEAPONS

Sword of the Spirit

"Take the sword of the Spirit, which is the word of God" (Ephesians 6:17b).

A sword is a thrusting, striking, or cutting weapon with a long blade having one or more cutting edges. It is a weapon of offense that is used to attack an enemy. The enemy in this case is satan and his hosts. When the enemy attacks us on any front, we use the other weapons for defense, to block the attack. When we are on the offensive, we attack him with the Word of God.

It is often said that the best form of defense is to attack. We cannot allow ourselves to be buffeted and attacked without response. We have to defend ourselves with the weapons of defense and attack the enemy with the Word of God.

Always remember, that the arm of flesh will fail, but absolute reliance on God will lead to total victory. The Spirit of God—the Holy Spirit—the third person of the Trinity—will expressly carry out the promises in the Word, as long as we study and rightly appropriate Scripture to work on our behalf.

The best example for us to follow is found in the gospels where Jesus was tempted by the devil (Matt. 4:1-11; Mark 1:12-13; Luke 4:1-13). In all three accounts, Jesus quoted the Word and said, "It is written." Jesus overcame the devil with the Word of God. Friend, resist the devil with the Word of God, and he will flee!

Satan is a remarkably crafty, and an extremely wicked being, but Jesus has already overcome him. In that victory, we still have the duty to study the Word and to enforce the will of God for our lives.

The Weapon of Prayer

"Praying always with all prayer and supplication in the Spirit, and watching thereunto with all perseverance and supplication for all the saints" (Eph. 6:18)

Prayer has its own precepts. Among them:

- praying to God (Heb. 11:6)

- praying in the name of Jesus (John 14:6)

- praying in the Spirit (Eph. 6:18)

- praying according to the will of God (1 John 5:14)

- praying in faith (Eph. 3:20; James 1:6)

- praying earnestly (Luke 6:12)

- praying without hypocrisy (Matt. 6:5)

Ephesians 6:18 also teaches us how to pray, when to pray, the type of prayers to pray and for whom to pray. Pray with "all prayer and supplication in the Spirit." "Pray always." Watch thereunto and pray for all saints. Furthermore, as you pray in the Spirit, the Holy Spirit helps you to pray about issues beyond your human understanding.

Prayer is a powerful weapon when we pray with petitions and supplications. We must stand in the gap on behalf of others, to ask that the will of God be fulfilled in their lives. With this in mind, we take on our duty to be alert and keep praying for all the saints.

CHAPTER SEVEN

DEFEATING THE ENEMY

"And Jesus being full of the Holy Ghost returned from Jordan, and was led by the Spirit into the wilderness, Being forty days tempted of the devil. And in those days he did eat nothing: and when they were ended, he afterward hungered. And the devil said unto him, If thou be the Son of God, command this stone that it be made bread. And Jesus answered him, saying, It is written, That man shall not live by bread alone, but by every word of God. And the devil, taking him up into an high mountain, shewed unto him all the kingdoms of the world in a moment of time. And the devil said unto him, All this power will I give thee, and the glory of them: for that is delivered unto me; and to whomsoever I will I give it. If thou therefore wilt worship me, all shall be thine. And Jesus answered and said unto him, Get thee behind me, Satan: for it is written, Thou shalt worship the Lord thy God, and him only shalt thou serve. And he brought him to Jerusalem, and set him on a pinnacle of the temple, and said unto him, If thou be the Son of God, cast thyself down from hence: For it is written, He shall give his angels charge over thee, to keep thee: And in their hands they shall bear thee up, lest at any time thou dash thy foot against a stone. And Jesus answering said unto him, It is said, Thou shalt not tempt the Lord thy God. And when the devil had ended all the temptation, he departed from him for a season.   And Jesus returned in the

power of the Spirit into Galilee: and there went out a fame of him through all the region round about." (Luke 4:1-14)

From the Holy Scriptures, we learn that our Lord Jesus Christ used five major keys of the kingdom to bind and defeat satan. He used the keys of fasting, prayer, submission, resistance and the Word.

Fasting

The Scripture says in, *"Being forty days tempted of the devil. And in those days He did eat nothing: and when they were ended, He afterward hungered."* (Luke 4:2) "He did eat nothing" means that He abstained from food which is carnal or fleshly—to be empowered spiritually. Fasting is a necessary tool and spiritual weapon every child of God must activate if the strong man is to be bound.

There is no substitute for the key of fasting. It is necessary to understand that various keys are meant for specific doors. You cannot use the key to the front door of the house to open the kitchen or the bedroom. Neither can you use the key to a Volkswagen to start a Mercedes. In the spiritual realm, specifically in the kingdom of God, various keys are meant for different functions. Different keys unlock the storehouses to different treasures of God.

Fasting unlocks the treasure of spiritual power. Our Lord Jesus Christ said, *"Howbeit this kind goeth not out but by prayer and fasting."* (Matt. 17:21) There are certain strong men that will not be bound except by fasting and prayer.

Activate the spiritual weapons of fasting and prayer, and you will be amazed at the results in your life.

Prayer

The second key employed by our Lord Jesus Christ, in His supreme example as author and finisher of our faith, is the powerful weapon of prayer. Prayer is communication with God. Communication is a two-way flow of information. Most people assume that prayer is just talking to God, but that is absolutely not the case. Prayer is talking to God, and God talking back to you.

No other spiritual weapon substitutes the place of fervent prayer. Prayer must be fervent, intensive, persistent, and effective: *"...The effectual fervent prayer of a righteous man availeth much. Elias was a man subject to like passions as we are, and he prayed earnestly that it might not rain: and it rained not on the earth by the space of three years and six months. And he prayed again, and the heaven gave rain, and the earth brought forth her fruit."* (James 5:16-18)

Jesus Christ, our High Priest, commands us to pray and not faint (Luke 18:1-8). The prayer that transcends the realm of the natural and penetrates the realm of the supernatural to bring into manifestation the purposes of God is agonizing, travailing prayer. It is endless: *"Likewise the Spirit also helpeth our infirmities: for we know not what we should pray for as we ought: but the Spirit itself maketh intercession for us with groanings which cannot be uttered.*

And he that searcheth the hearts knoweth what is the mind of the Spirit, because he maketh intercession for the saints according to the will of God." (Romans 8:26-27) Through prayer, we fight the good fight of faith and the strong man is bound.

Employ the weapon of endless, ceaseless prayers with the Word of God and all satanic obstacles will give way for a full manifestation and demonstration of God's purposes for your life.

Submission

Another way by which our Lord Jesus Christ overcame satan is through submission. Submission is willingly obeying instructions and giving of oneself to a worthy cause—in this case, it is the Word of God.

In submission to God's Word, every attitude of rebellion, stubbornness or disobedience is absolutely eliminated. According to the Scriptures, nobody can avenge any form of disobedience when obedience is incomplete. *"And having in a readiness to revenge all disobedience, when your obedience is fulfilled."* (2 Corinthians 10:6)

Scripture also says, *"Submit yourself therefore to God. Resist the devil, and he will flee."* (James 4:7) Beloved, you can never give satan commands for him to obey when you are not in obedience to God.

The story of Jesus and the centurion in the gospel according to Matthew gives us insight about what we are discussing.

"And when Jesus was entered into Capernaum, there came unto him a centurion, beseeching him, And saying, Lord, my servant lieth at home sick of the palsy, grievously tormented. And Jesus saith unto him, I will come and heal him. The centurion answered and said, Lord, I am not worthy that thou shouldest come under my roof: but speak the word only, and my servant shall be healed. For I am a man under authority, having soldiers under me: and I say to this man, Go, and he goeth; and to another, Come, and he cometh; and to my servant, Do this, and he doeth it. When Jesus heard it, he marvelled, and said to them that followed, Verily I say unto you, I have not found so great faith, no, not in Israel." (Matthew 8:5-10)

In verse nine, the centurion acknowledged that he was a man under authority. Being under authority is an attitude of submission. The absence of this vital virtue in the lives of the people of God has denied them the ability to bind the strong man.

There are three different kinds of authority—spiritual, civil, and domestic. Rebellion against any of these authorities is rebellion against God (Romans 13:1). Remember that the devil, who was previously Lucifer, was the first among God's creatures to rebel. That is why we have sin in the world today. Because of this initial experience of rebellion, God does not tolerate it on any level.

If you are going to be able to overcome satan and his demons, you must walk in absolute submission to the Word and the will of God at every stage and level of your life.

Submission is an indispensable weapon in binding the strong man.

Resistance

Resistance is also a key that our Lord and Savior Jesus Christ used. The word resistance, biblically speaking, means: to set against, to withstand, to stand firm against, to strive against, to oppose or to rage battle against.

This is exactly what our Master and King did to the devil during the temptation in the wilderness. In spite of all the tricks and temptations of the enemy, Jesus Christ, our supreme example, withstood the enemy. He steadfastly resisted the enemy at every point of the battle. This attitude of our King and Supreme Conqueror did not occur only during the temptation in the wilderness, but was a lifestyle He maintained throughout His earthly ministry.

If the apostle and high priest of our profession had to resist the enemy every step of the way, you and I need to do the same even more so. The Scripture says, *"Be sober, be vigilant; because your adversary the devil, as a roaring lion, walketh about seeking whom he may devour: whom resist steadfast in the faith, knowing that the same afflictions are accomplished in your brethren that are in the world."* (1 Peter 5:8-9)

The apostle Peter encourages believers to stand firm against the enemy. Throughout the Scriptures, anyone who had made a mark for God in his or her generation had to resist the enemy steadfastly.

You need to apply the key of resistance to overcome satan. It is not just short-term, cozy, relaxed prayer that deals with the strong man! It is steadfast resistance coupled with all the other keys. You must refuse to be what the enemy wants you to be, and you must insist on God's prophetic agenda for your life to come to pass.

The Word of God

The Word of God is manifested in different dimensions. It is given to us as the written Word, the spoken Word, and the living Word. Jesus Christ, the Son of God, who walked on the shores of Galilee, is the living Word. The Scriptures say;

"In the beginning was the Word, and Word was with God, and the Word was God . . . And the Word was made flesh and dwelt among us, (and we beheld His glory, the glory as of the only begotten of the Father), full of grace and truth." (John 1:1, 14)

"The Word was made flesh and dwelt among us…" talks of the incarnation of the Word of God as the living Word.

The spoken Word is the Word of God released as a two-edged sword from the mouth of the believer. The Bible says it is active and alive.

The written Word is the *logos*, that which has been recorded in the Scriptures.

All these manifestations of the Word of God are powerful and contain all the attributes of God. The Scriptures declare that, *"For in Him dwelleth all the fullness of the Godhead bodily. And ye are complete in Him which is the head of all principality and power."* (Col. 2:9-10) *"Jesus Christ is the same yesterday, today, and forever."* (Heb. 13:8)

The final key that Jesus Christ, the living Word, used to bind the strong man were the keys of the written Word and the spoken Word.

Anywhere, anytime, and under any situation or circumstance that satan and his demons are confronted with the Word of God, they are totally overpowered. It is written, *"the light shineth in darkness, and the darkness cannot comprehend the power of the light."* (John 1:5) Evil spirits and/or demons will always be bound when the Word of God is released against them. Too often believers pray, shout, and make a lot of noise; but they do not speak the Word.

In the book of Matthew, the centurion asked our Lord Jesus Christ not to worry Himself with coming over to the house; but to just speak the word, and his servant would be healed. Nothing is comparable with the spoken Word. Heaven and earth may pass, but the Word abides forever. *"Forever, O Lord, Thy Word is settled in heaven."* (Psalm 119:89)

The centurion had the revelation of authority. He knew that authority was to have one's words and commands obeyed. He also knew that the Lord Jesus Christ, the living Word, only had to release the spoken word, because He was (and still is) the One who has all authority. Sickness, or any other oppression, simply has to obey Him.

In Mark 5, the Bible speaks of a man bound with unclean spirits. This man was uncontrollable. On many occasions, he had been bound with chains; but he would break the chains and cut himself. His condition was hopeless. A legion of demons indwelt him.. However, when Jesus Christ (the living Word) approached him and questioned the authority of the strong man that had bound this man; immediately, the strong man began to tremble, was driven out, and the man was clothed in his right senses. *"And they came over unto the other side of the sea, into the country of the Gadarenes. And when he was come out of the ship, immediately there met him out of the tombs a man with an unclean spirit, Who had his dwelling among the tombs; and no man could bind him, no, not with chains: Because that he had been often bound with fetters and chains, and the chains had been plucked asunder by him, and the fetters broken in pieces: neither could any man tame him. And always, night and day, he was in the mountains, and in the tombs, crying, and cutting himself with stones. But when he saw Jesus afar off, he ran and worshipped him, And cried with a loud voice, and said, What have I to do with thee, Jesus, thou Son of the most high God? I adjure thee by God, that thou torment me not. For he said unto him, Come out of the man, thou unclean spirit. And he asked him, What is thy name? And he answered, saying, My name is Legion: for we are many. And he besought him much that he would not send them away out of the country. Now there was there nigh unto the mountains a great herd of swine feeding. And all the devils besought him, saying, Send us into the swine, that we may enter into them. And forthwith Jesus gave them leave. And the unclean spirits went out, and entered into the swine: and the herd ran violently down a steep place into the sea, (they were about two thousand;) and were choked in the sea. And they that fed the swine fled, and told it in the city, and in the country. And they went out to see what it was that was done. And they come to Jesus, and see him that was possessed with the devil, and had the legion, sitting, and clothed, and in his right mind: and they were afraid."* (Mark 5:1-15)

Enforce the Word of God, overcome the enemy, and obtain notable miracles in every area of your life. *"This book of the law shall not depart out of thy mouth; but thou shalt meditate therein day and night, that thou mayest observe to do according to all that is written therein: for thou shalt make thy way prosperous, and then thou shalt have good successs."* (Joshua 1:8)

In conclusion, the Bible says, *"And they said, Believe on the Lord Jesus Christ, and thou shalt be saved, and thy house."* (Act 16:31)

Let us not be ignorant of the devices of the enemy. Trust in the word of the Lord, have faith in it, apply it always and you shall be an overcomer.

There are powers behind the scenes!

Action Chapel, Spintex Road, Ghana

Service Times

Sunday 1st: 6am – 8am

Sunday 2nd: 8am – 10am

Sunday 3rd: 10am – 12pm

Sunday 4th: 6pm – 8:30pm

Wednesday Teaching Service: 5:30pm – 8:30pm

Thursday Dominion Hour: 9am – 12pm

Friday All Night: 12am – 5am

For Action branches, fellowships, and other church activities, please contact the church office on

+233.302.745.000: *Church Office*

Or visit www.actionchapel.net

You can also connect with us on

Dominion Television,

Channel 5 on the MultiTV platform.

115

Other Books by the

Archbishop Nicholas Duncan-Williams

- The Incredible Power of a Praying Woman
- When Mothers Pray
- Turning Pain to Power
- Enforcing Prophetic Decrees
- Praying through the Promises of God
- Binding the Strong Man
- Divine Timing
- Destined to Make an Impact
- The Supernatural Power of a Praying Man
- Worship A Secret Weapon
- The Lamp Devotional

And much more……

Contact Dominion Bookshop on
+233.54.375.6884 for more information.

For more information on
Archbishop Nicholas Duncan-Williams
please visit us online or contact
the office closest to you.

AFRI CA

www.actionchapel.net
www.actionchapel.tv: live streaming
+233.54.375.6884: Bookstore
+233.307.011.851: *Church Office*

EUROPE

www.actionchapel.org.uk
Tel: + 44.0208.952.0626

NORTH AMERICA

Prayer Summit International
www.prayersummitinternational.org

Action Worship Center, Maryland
www.awclaurel.org

Action Chapel VA, Virginia
www.actionchapelva.org

Action Chapel Baltimore
www.actionchapelbaltimore.com

51613762R20066

Made in the USA
San Bernardino, CA
03 September 2019